LI KA-SHING

&

CHEUNG KONG HOLDINGS

A BUSINESS AND LIFE BIOGRAPHY

Published by
LID Publishing Limited
The Record Hall, Studio 304,
16-16a Baldwins Gardens,
London EC1N 7RJ, UK

info@lidpublishing.com
www.lidpublishing.com

A member of:

BPR ✹
businesspublishersroundtable.com

Published in collaboration with the China Translation & Publishing House (a member of the China Publishing Group Corporation)
Translated by Dr. Zhu Yuan, Xu Kun, Sun Shihao, Hao Jinxi

 China Translation and Publishing House

© LID Publishing Limited, 2021
© China Translation and Publishing House, 2021

Printed in the United States
ISBN: 978-1-912555-46-8
ISBN: 978-1-911671-76-3 (ebook)

Illustration: Benson Koo
Cover and page design: Caroline Li

LI KA-SHING

&

CHEUNG KONG HOLDINGS

A BUSINESS AND LIFE BIOGRAPHY

BY **YAN QICHENG**

MADRID | MEXICO CITY | LONDON
NEW YORK | BUENOS AIRES
BOGOTA | SHANGHAI | NEW DELHI

CONTENTS

INTRODUCTION

'The Yangtze River incorporates every stream, so it flows over 10,000 li.'

On the Geladandong Peak in the Dangla Mountains, towering over the Tibetan Plateau, the azure sky is like a mirror and the ice and snow are like silver. What a fairyland, beautiful and tranquil.

In the sun, life is born. A little stream gurgles, zigzagging under ice and snow, like a young seedling breaking ground. It flows like a thin snake, feeble and soft, powerlessly down the slope, along the valley and towards the plain. In the process, numerous streams and rivers join in, and they gradually merge and become one giant river, sweeping over half of China.

This is the mighty Cheung Kong – the Yangtze River of 10,000 li (5,000 kilometres). It has been an inspiration, and a symbol of inclusiveness, determination and strength, for the man whose story we're about to tell.

Following the death of his father, 14-year-old Li Ka-shing dropped out of school and became an apprentice in a local Hong Kong teahouse, cleaning and serving tea at the nearby Zhongnan Watch Company. He soon began learning how to repair watches, how to do business and how to conduct himself. In those days, some said he was feeble bodied, with dull eyes. Many thought he could not achieve much.

In this mundane world, like a weak leaf of grass, he struggled and lived in wind and rain. Two years later, he was hired as a clerk in a watch shop, where he learned how to repair and assemble watches and clocks. He eventually decided to make his living as a salesman for a hardware factory. And then, due to his remarkable sales achievements, he became the general manager of a plastic factory.

In 1950, pinching and scraping, the 22-year-old Li Ka-shing saved $7,000 and set up his Cheung Kong Plastic Factory in Hong Kong's Shau Kei Wan neighborhood. The weak grass grew tall and firm, and he started a new round of personal development.

Five years later, in a flash of keen business insight, Li Ka-shing recognized the magical resemblance between plastic flowers and real flowers. After careful thought and investigation, he decided to produce plastic flowers at his factory. When his creations entered the market, people marveled over their color, shape and durability. Very soon, his flowers took off and were soon sold all over the world. They brought Li Ka-shing huge profit and success, helping this would-be Chinese tycoon gain a firmer footing.

Ever since then, Li Ka-shing has exerted enormous influence on Hong Kong and Kowloon, where he became known as 'The King of Plastic Flowers.' He also became a star personality in business and politics.

Two years after starting to produce plastic flowers, Li Ka-shing renamed his factory Cheung Kong Industries and established its headquarters in Hong Kong's North Point district.

In 1958, he completed the construction of a 12-storey office building. In 1960, the company's second building rose in Hong Kong's Chai Wan industrial area. This was a landmark event. Why? It proclaimed Li Ka-shing's ambition to move into the property business.

The Yangtze River performs innumerable twists and turns, rolling forwards ceaselessly in the valleys of the Yunnan-Guizhou Plateau, incorporating the Minjiang River, Tuojiang River, Jialingjiang River and Wujiang River into a gigantic force and rushing towards the Jianghan Plain like a giant dragon. By the late 1950s, Li Ka-shing and his Cheung Kong Property Holdings Limited had also become such a dragon.

Faced with the ups and downs of the markets, business opportunities and competition, Li Ka-shing, with his unique economic vision and keen business sense, always seemed to make the right move at the right time. Indeed, he gradually consolidated his business empire through a series of ever-greater achievements and acquisitions.

In 1967, amid labour disputes and large-scale demonstrations against British colonial rule, Hong Kong was in chaos, with squabbles and riots breaking out everywhere. From Tsim Sha Tsui to Mong Kok – spanning the entire Kowloon peninsula – property prices plummeted. However, Li Ka-shing continued purchasing property, accumulating abundant land for the future development of Cheung Kong Property Holdings Limited.

This was a masterstroke that he undoubtedly felt proud of. In Hong Kong, where every inch of land was as precious as gold, such acquisitions gave wings to Li Ka-shing and Cheung Kong Property Holdings Limited. By then the former teahouse apprentice was being hailed as the richest man in Asia and a giant of the business world.

The following were landmark moments for Li Ka-shing:

- In 1979, the purchase of 22.4% of the British firm Hutchison Whampoa
- In 1984, the purchase of Hongkong Electric Company, Limited
- In 1986, the purchase of half of the Canadian oil company Husky Energy
- In 2010, together with CK Infrastructure Holdings, Limited, Hongkong Electric Company, Limited, the Li Ka-shing Foundation and the Li Ka-shing Overseas Foundation, Li bid on and purchased parts of the British power grid services as a subordinate of Électricité de France, paying £5.775 billion
- In 2012, *Forbes* magazine's 'The World's Billionaires' list ranked Li Ka-shing Number 9 globally and Number 1 in Asia, with wealth of approximately $30 billion

His business sphere expanded from plastics and property to many sectors, such as electric power, ports, telecommunications, water supply and retail. His four flagship businesses included Cheung Kong Property Holdings Limited, Hopewell Holdings Limited, CK Infrastructure Holdings Limited and Power Assets Holdings Limited.

Given his extraordinary success, some began calling Li Ka-shing 'Superman Li.'

Liu Baiyu, the famous Chinese writer, gives a splendid description of the Yangtze River in his *Three Days on the Yangtze River*, particularly elaborating on the beauty of the Three Gorges. On Qutang Gorge, he said, "Rivers meet at Wanzhou and Fuling, and they all compete to pass Qutang Gorge. Two or three junks work their way upstream against the current, their oars moving rhythmically, reminiscent of the flapping wings of birds."

How vivid! What profound associations! Magnificent? Romantic? Yes ... but with these words he actually told us more about competition, exertion and struggle.

The Yangtze River, starting from a little pond, absorbing water from the sky and the Earth's glaciers, runs to the Yunnan-Guizhou Plateau, dashes through formidable barriers in Sichuan, passes the Three Gorges, and leaves Jingmen, in Hubei, far behind.

Along its way, Liu Baiyu tells us, the mighty current breaks through all obstacles, experiences "high mountains, precipitous gorges, and thunder and storm," faces the "most perilous pass of Qutang Gorge," passes the "dreary and desolate Wushan Mountain and Wu Gorge," and eventually reaches the "boundless expanse of the wChu fields."

This is a writer with great imagination crying out: What a wonderful world! This is true life!

But an entrepreneur like Li Ka-shing must be confident and commanding in every step, calmly facing difficulties with full concentration and a sense of balance that's incomprehensible to others. Any hesitation can lead to the loss of his fortune. A rash decision can lead to a precipitous fall from the top.

This too is life, which recalls yesterday but points towards the future, and which envisions tomorrow ... but uncertainty always remains.

Many years later, overlooking Victoria Harbour from atop the headquarters of Cheung Kong Holdings in central Hong Kong, did Li Ka-shing recall the trials and tribulations of his youth? Did he think of the hardship he had endured? Did he stand in awe of his own exciting life?

This we do not know, but we do know that he is a winner in the game of life, a giant of the business world, and one of the richest men in Asia.

Yet, no one in the world can achieve success with complete ease. No matter how encouraging and inspiring, a legend is only a legend. Every winner must be solidly grounded and attached to the motherland, just like the Yangtze River, incorporating every stream and every river and rushing towards the ocean over 10,000 li.

In addition to his unique business vision, shrewd insight and resolute decisions, Li Ka-shing and Cheung Kong Holdings needed to maintain open-mindedness, magnanimity and integrity, along with passion, sincerity and a simple heart dedicated to always doing right.

Now, let us start at the beginning and learn about the man who is Li Ka-shing.

CHAPTER

1

INITIATION

1. THE POOR LAD

Bright like fireworks but ruthless like a demon! The sweet night sky of Hong Kong was bombarded into fragments as this free port was attacked by the Japanese army at the end of 1941.

Li Ka-shing's family, who had moved to Hong Kong from Guangdong Province to escape the ravages of World War II, were once again faced with the Japanese aggressors' indiscriminate bombing. Soon after, the British surrendered and the Japanese seized full control of Hong Kong.

For the rest of the war, the Japanese occupation of Hong Kong resulted in closed factories and scarce supplies. As the hardships mounted, 14-year-old Li Ka-shing had to be separated from his family. His mother, Chong Bik Kam, returned to their home town of Teochew, some 300 kilometres north of Hong Kong, with his younger brother and sister. Before she left, she caressed Li Ka-shing's head and told him over and over again: "Listen to your uncle and your father, and wait for me."

Despite his young appearance, the hardships of life taught Li to behave like an adult. "Don't worry, mom, father and I will always be together," said Li to his mother, with tears in his eyes.

His father, Li Wan King, had been well educated as a child and had worked as a teacher in Teochew. But in wartime Hong Kong, how could it be possible to find a peaceful position in a classroom? Eventually, he could only work as a clerk in a small shop, at the recommendation of Li Ka-shing's uncle.

There, he witnessed the people of Hong Kong enthusiastically donating money to support the resistance effort on the mainland. Without money, it was impossible to mount any sort of defense against a foreign invasion. Therefore, Li Wan King, a descendant of Confucius and Mencius, believed in saving the nation through education. He came to feel that industry could also help in a big way. He once expressed this view to young Li Ka-shing, which may have planted a seed that became sown in the boy's heart. Once the opportunity came, it would take root, sprout and thrive.

Soon after Li's mother left, due to the scarcity of food and other goods, his father was stricken with tuberculosis.

With the ravages of war, his father's condition worsened day by day, until he could no longer get out of bed. Still, he refused to take medication, as he tried to save money for Li Ka-shing's tuition.

Even after all these years, whenever Li looks back on those days, tears fill his eyes. His father's love, like the mountain gorges that give strength to the descending river, gave the young boy the strength to forge ahead.

Tuberculosis at that time almost always meant death, and when Li Ka-shing's uncle, Chong Ching On, finally forced the boy's father into the hospital, it was too late. Moments before his death, too weak to utter a word, Li Wan King held Li Ka-shing's hands tightly and gazed at him. Li Ka-shing understood his father's dying wish, and he swore by heaven: "I will give our family a good life!"

Hearing this, Li Wan King closed his eyes and was gone forever.

And so began Li Ka-shing's initiation into the trials and tribulations of life. He encountered two swindlers. The men claimed they could sell the teenager a grave for his father's burial, and he made a deposit. But Li Ka-shing was suspicious, so he asked to see the cemetery in person. The men thought the child was easy to cheat and were ready to dump him on the way. But they could not shake off Li, so they took him to the cemetery. The two whispered in the Hakka dialect, plotting to go dig up a body and sell the stolen grave to him.

What they did not expect was that Li Ka-shing, whose family was from Teochew, knew Hakka. The boy was trembling with anger when he heard their conversation. How could there be such shameless people in this world? But he knew that as a thin teenager he was no match for the men. They could easily overpower him. Therefore, he said to them as calmly as possible: "I have heard all your words. Don't bother! The deposit is all yours, and I will find another seller."

Later, Li Ka-shing's father was buried in the Sandy Ridge Cemetery near Luohu, a northern district of Hong Kong.

However, this incident had a profound influence on Li. From then on, he warned himself to never make money against one's conscience. This would become the motto of his life.

Now that his father had passed away, it seemed that Li Ka-shing was all alone. In fact, that was not the case. There was still a powerful man standing behind him – his uncle, Chong Ching On. When Li Ka-shing's family had left Teochew, they'd gone to Hong Kong because the uncle was there for Li; Chong Ching On was like another mountain, as his father had been, standing behind him and giving him support.

If his father taught him integrity and honesty, his uncle taught him the shrewdness of businessmen and the diligence of migrant workers. They both taught him the benefits of simplicity, maintaining a low profile and helping others.

Without his uncle, it would be hard to imagine how Li Ka-shing could have survived, and gone on to achieve what he did.

To Li, Chong Ching On would go on to assume another identity – as his father-in-law – but that is a later story.

Early on, the uncle stood back and watched the frail young man, letting him struggle in the crowd. Only when Li Ka-shing was in the most difficult of situations did he lend a helping hand. All the ideas, all the difficulties, and all the advances and retreats were decided by young Li Ka-shing himself.

This was because Chong Ching On believed that one had to walk through difficulties in life on his own. That was where one's skills and character were honed. He did the same with other family members as they made their way.

When Li Ka-shing and his family first arrived in Hong Kong, Chong Ching On immediately vacated his house for them to live in. He also provided them with financial aid, to help them resettle and survive. However, he did not give Li Wan King a job in his successful Zhongnan Watch Company, nor did he arrange for Li Ka-shing to work there following his father's death.

His company was large and needed many hands – employing Li Ka-shing would not have been a problem – but he did not offer a position, leaving the teenager to make his own decisions.

This may seem heartless, but there is a deeper emotion here. Like the rest of the family, Chong Ching On was from Teochew and the people there are unique in their ways.

Teochew occupies a small corner of northeastern Guangdong Province. It is famous for being the home of travelling Chinese people. Since ancient times, countless Teochew have sailed to Southeast Asia, where they achieved great things in strange lands. Teochew not only has its own dialect but also its own distinctive cuisine, architecture and music. In short, the place has its own unique culture and style.

In addition, the Teochew people respect hard work, rather than vanity. They are never satisfied with the status quo and always try to forge ahead. They are perhaps the most hardworking group among Chinese people.

Chong Ching On, who embodied these typical Teochew values and traits, wanted to see his nephew struggle ahead and make it on his own.

However, Li Ka-shing was now just 15 years old and knew little about the world. Nevertheless, without his father, and owing to his uncle's insistence that he make his own way, he had to independently carry the burden of life. Just like a young bird in the jungle, deprived of his father's protection, he had no other option but to fly.

Fortunately, Li Ka-shing had the Teochew people's blood flowing through his veins. After having his father buried, he did not ask his uncle to give him a job at the watch company. Rather, he began to rush about Hong Kong's shops, restaurants, hotels and factories, searching for a job so that he could get by.

By 1943, under Japanese control, Hong Kong had lost all its businesses. Nearly a million people fled, leaving behind only 600,000 residents. One can imagine how difficult it was to make a living under such circumstances.

There were only a few pedestrians in the main street, and buses took half a day to come. Wind blew and garbage whirled. The Japanese soldiers on patrol, stamping in their boots and flashing their bayonets, made people shudder.

Li Ka-shing's first thought was of his fellow Teochew countrymen, who were famous for their unity. No matter where they are, they organize their own associations. However, at that time, under such atrocious circumstances, the Teochew were struggling to take care of themselves.

But Li Ka-shing thought of an immigrant shopkeeper with the surname Huang. Li called him Uncle Huang.

Years earlier the two had been neighbours, living in Beimen Street in Teochew. When Li was young, Uncle Huang was a student of Li Ka-shing's other uncle, Li Wan-Cheong. So, they were old family friends.

Full of hope, Li Ka-shing found Huang's grocery shop, but he was shocked by the scene that greeted him. The door of the shop was closed and surrounded by garbage, and the signboard that used to be so conspicuous was nowhere to be seen.

Without entering, Li Ka-shing knew the shop was closed. As for where Uncle Huang was, he did not know.

Such was Hong Kong in 1943 under the occupation of Japanese imperialists. All trades and professions had withered, and the people had no livelihood. In a flash, disappointment came over Li, and he felt like he was falling into an ice cave. He was so depressed that he lost strength in his legs and struggled to get home.

His cousin, Chong Yuet Ming, came to see him. On that cold day, her beautiful eyes were like fire to him. Looking at Li's red and swollen feet, Chong Yuet Ming brought him warm water. She told him that success lay in perseverance. Li bit his lip, tears swirling in his eyes. He nodded to his cousin in silence.

In the piercing wind, his cousin's fiery eyes warmed Li Ka-shing, and became a motivation for him to keep on striving.

It was not romantic love, but he stored the warmth of this familiar love in his chest like it was sunshine, allowing him to fend off the cold seeping into his skin.

2. TEAHOUSE BOY

Young Li Ka-shing did not know that Uncle Chong was watching him. Yet when Chong Yuet Ming returned home, he was the first to ask her about Li. Hearing of the boy's predicament, he sipped Kungfu tea and remained silent.

Li Ka-shing continued to travel along the streets of Hong Kong, incessantly looking for jobs of any sort. Unfortunately, most shops were closed, and the businesses that had managed to survive did not need employees.

Finally, he came to a teahouse called Chunming. It was located at Sai Ying Pun, an area in the Western district of Hong Kong. Its boss was Li Ka-mao, who also hailed from Teochew. Moreover, back home in Teochew, he had known Li Ka-shing's father quite well.

Seeing the poor teenager walking into the teahouse, Li Ka-mao knew at first glance that he was not a customer. Sure enough, Li Ka-shing bowed politely and explained his purpose in the Teochew dialect.

Li Ka-mao wanted to say no, but hearing Li Ka-shing's familiar accent, he asked a few more questions. When he realized that this lean, hungry-looking boy was Li Wan King's son, and that the father had passed away, sorrow overcame him. After all, the kind and learned Li Wan King had enjoyed a good reputation in the village. Seeing young Li Ka-shing alone in this strange land, Li Ka-mao felt compassion.

Finally, he said, "Well, first find yourself someone to vouch for you, and you can come to my teahouse to work."

The good news almost made Li Ka-shing jump with joy. However, he just took a step back, made a solemn salute and bid farewell to the manager.

Back home, Li Ka-shing pondered over who should provide his reference. Uncle Chong would be the best, he thought, as he was both a Teochew man and the boss of a watch company. He definitely had the credentials.

Just then, footsteps sounded in the courtyard. It was Chong Ching On and his daughter, Chong Yuet Ming. They brought a bag of rice and a stack of cash. Uncle Chong patted Li Ka-shing on the head and remained silent. He knew about his nephew's efforts to secure a job. "No need to run around the city looking for a job anymore," he told the boy. "Just come to my watch company. We need some extra hands after all."

Li Ka-shing looked up and saw the shining eyes of his cousin. Of course, he was happy to hear this, as his uncle's company would be better than the teahouse. Not only would the working conditions be better, but learning clock repairs was appealing to him, as the skills were imported from the West and were very popular.

However, Li Ka-shing did not answer immediately. Chong Ching On was a little surprised by this. He looked down at his nephew, only to find that he had already started shaking his head. Finally, Li spoke: "Thank you, uncle, but I've found a job today," he said. "I just need someone to vouch for me. Will you be my reference?"

Caught off guard at first, Chong Ching On asked about the other job offer in detail. At last, he replied, "OK, I will vouch for you. The teahouse is a melting pot of all walks of life. Working there, you can learn a lot of things other than mechanical techniques."

Perhaps Chong Ching On had already recognized Li Ka-shing's uniqueness and hoped that he would become an outstanding businessman. The teahouse was indeed a good place to experience life, but Uncle Chong could never have imagined that Li was going to become the richest man in Asia.

Still, he agreed to Li's choice and to providing his reference. Chong Yuet Ming took out a small amulet she'd gotten in the temple, hoping her cousin would be safe forever. And so, Li Ka-shing became a teahouse boy, who served drinks, swept the floor, ran errands and ushered guests.

A teahouse in southern China is, in effect, a restaurant. Besides tea, it also serves many delicacies. The so-called 'drinking morning tea,' is actually to have breakfast. Therefore, a teahouse has to open at 6am every morning, and it closes late at night.

Li Ka-shing would often arrive at the teahouse before dawn to tidy up tables and chairs, and then wait for guests to come. No matter who they were, he would greet them and see them off warmly. The guests came from different backgrounds; everyone dressed differently and spoke differently. Li Ka-shing observed them all, and learned to judge their occupations, hobbies and even personalities from their speech and behavior.

His observations about people often proved to be precisely right. If the teahouse had given Li Ka-shing his first lesson in life, it taught him the art of 'knowing people.'

Chong Ching On was not upset by Li Ka-shing's decision not to work in his own company. On the contrary, he was very pleased because it was a sign of his nephew's maturity. Chong gave Li an alarm clock so that he could avoid being late. As a result, he got up at 5am every morning, bathed and then immediately headed for the teahouse.

On the way, Li created a game for himself that he called 'continuous transcendence.' It involved continually passing the people walking in front of him. This made him travel with vigorous strides, and he became accustomed to speed. Working in the teahouse for a year, he was never late and he never left early. Punctuality took root inside his mind from that moment on.

What motivated him? Was it mere perseverance? Or was it the heavy burden of poverty, with the livelihood of his family at stake?

Later, when talking about this experience to his son, Li Ka-shing said, "At that time, my biggest wish was to sleep soundly for three days and nights."

On one occasion, Li Ka-shing was fascinated by the small talk of tea drinkers and forgot to refill guests' cups. Hearing the loud reproach from a senior waiter, he grabbed a big teapot and scrambled to the table. In a hurry, he tripped over a customer's foot, and the hot tea was spilled on the hem of the customer's trousers.

Li Ka-shing's face turned white with fear, and not knowing what to do, he simply stood there. It was a serious accident, as a few days before a waiter had spilled water on a customer who was a member of the 'triad white paper fan' gang. The boss personally made an apology, and the waiter knelt on the spot to apologize, but he was fired.

Fearing a similar fate , Li Ka-shing started to feel dizzy.

Just as the boss, Li Ka-mao, rushed over to apologize, the guest brushed the wet hem of his trousers and said softly, "I don't blame him. I tripped him." The customer patted Li Ka-shing on the shoulder and comforted him softly: "It's fine, young man."

Afterwards, Li Ka-mao warned Li Ka-shing: "You must be careful in your future work. In case of any mishap, you should immediately make an apology to the customer and try to make big problems smaller and small ones gone. This time the guest was kind-hearted, but if you encountered someone mean, you would be in big trouble. In a teahouse, customers are like our parents offering us food and clothes, so we must be careful."

This incident had a great impact on Li Ka-shing, teaching him to be more rigorous and careful, and very much informing his style of dealing with situations. The generosity of that customer was engraved in the young man's heart, and to some extent it influenced his whole life. Even after he became the rich and powerful owner of Cheung Kong, he still reflected upon it. He once said to his friends, "Although it was a small matter, it means a lot to me. If I could find that customer, I would see to it that he has a happy life in return for his great kindness."

Working as a waiter in the teahouse for a year, Li had only that one mishap. Afterwards, he worked harder and harder, spending 15 hours a day at the job. Soon, the boss came to recognize his diligence and hard work. He got a pay raise and was promoted to senior waiter.

By this time, Li Ka-shing was 16 years old and felt that his days of running up and down with the teapot should be over.

His father, Li Wan King, had been a teacher. He advocated the ways of Confucius and Mencius all his life and liked learning. He once wanted his son to follow this path, but in Hong Kong, Li Wan King found that many successful fellow countrymen, including Chong Ching On, took another path. Li Wan King's thinking changed, and Li Ka-shing gradually came to understand this other path: to make money in business and help the country prosper through industry.

At the teahouse, Li Ka-shing had acquired many skills, including how to observe people and deal with different personalities and backgrounds. The secret, he discovered, was not to be glib, but to be compatible with people. Without this ability, it is easy to be distant in your interactions, which will bore people and make it difficult to forge relationships. Letting people trust you, understand you and feel your credibility is the crucial first step in dealing with people.

Li Ka-shing was confident that he had acquired this skill from his time at the teahouse, and he began to think about what he should do in the future. He decided that he would pursue business, earn more money, and achieve what he had pledged to his father – to make a good life for his family.

After deliberate consideration, he respectfully resigned from the teahouse. Li Ka-mao, of course, could not have foreseen that this frail youth would become a Hong Kong business tycoon, but he was sorry to see him leave. After all, he had mastered the ways of the teahouse, and his skilled service had been recognized by the guests.

Li Ka-mao patted him on the shoulder and said, "Well, Chunming always welcomes you."

This time, Uncle Chong did not hesitate and immediately agreed to employ Li Ka-shing at the Zhongnan Watch Company.

3. THE WATCH SHOP

Zhongnan Watch Company was the crystallization of Chong Ching On's painstaking, lifelong efforts.

At the beginning, it was a small factory that produced watchbands. Due to its high quality and low prices, it quickly gained a firm foothold. Later, the company acted as an agent for Swiss watch brands and developed repair and assembly technology, helping it grow stronger.

Seeing his nephew's hard work and diligence, Chong Ching On was very satisfied. He already felt that Li Ka-shing was fit for business, but he did not know how far he would go. Therefore, he still used the old way to train Li Ka-shing – to hone one's mind and character through hardship.

Li started at the watch company as a young apprentice. He was not allowed to do clock repairs or assembling, but was expected to complete chores, sweep the floor, boil and serve tea, and run errands. No one else there knew that this diligent little apprentice was boss Chong Ching On's nephew.

Li Ka-shing never talked much. He just worked hard and was very considerate. Whenever the master felt hot, Li would provide him with a comforting towel; whenever he felt thirsty, Li would bring him a cup of tea. As long as Li Ka-shing was there, the workshop would always be clean. The young apprentice was never lazy, but rather diligent like a clock, always ticking away.

Over time, everyone at the company came to like him. Experienced technicians offered to teach him, and he learned their skills very quickly. His intelligence and drive helped him learn almost everything about watch assembly and repair. Yet he was not boastful or proud. He owed all his knowledge and achievements to the repair masters.

Chong Ching On once commented, "Li Ka-shing's father died early, so he matured earlier than his peers. He thinks and behaves mostly like an adult."

Li had earned a place in his uncle's heart and was well respected by all of the company's employees. They still didn't know Li Ka-shing's relationship with Chong Ching On, but they told the boss that the young man was clever and diligent. With just a glance at other people's faces, they said, he knows what they want to do, and he immediately takes the initiative to help.

Seeing and hearing this, Chong Ching On was quite pleased ... and soon Li Ka-shing was a successful clockmaker.

In August of 1945, the Japanese surrendered. People who had escaped from Hong Kong during the war were soon returning at the rate of 100,000 a month. Li Ka-shing's mother returned to the city with his younger brother and sister. Only then did his mother learn about his father's death. Her eyes were full of tears and she paid tribute to Li Wan King.

Looking at Li Ka-shing, though, his mother found much consolation – her son had become a grown man. His shoulders were broad, his eyes were glowing with youthful spirit, and his sturdiness made Chong Bik Kam especially gratified. Uncle Chong Ching assured her that her 17-year-old son was perfectly capable of bearing the burden of a family.

As Hong Kong recovered from the war, everything was waiting to be revitalized. Chong Ching On, ever the smart businessman, smelled coming opportunities, expanded the scale of his watch company and opened new shops. During the company's expansion, Li Ka-shing was promoted to a clerk's position at a watch shop in Kao Sheng Street.

Being a clerk was nothing like being a teahouse boy. He didn't have to sweep the floor and serve tea, but he had to sell, and sell, and sell – selling watches and clocks, and selling repairs and other services.

Due to his experience in the teahouse, he could judge customers' occupations, hobbies, character and more from their clothes and manners the moment they walked into the shop. As a result, he knew exactly what they needed. For example, when someone walked in looking for nothing in particular, but touching his own wrist, Li Ka-shing immediately knew that the man was there for his watch to be repaired. He would step forwards and take the watch, explaining its characteristics and operation. In a moment, he could figure out the damaged part and answer the customer's questions.

Before long, he became the top salesperson in the company.

Later, the clerk who worked with Li told reporters: "Ka-shing came to the Kao Sheng shop as the youngest clerk. At first nobody took him seriously, but soon they all looked at him with special respect. He knew everything about clocks and watches, like a man who has been working in this trade for many years. No one could believe that he actually studied for only a few months. At that time, we all thought that he would become a skillful craftsman and a standard watchmaker. But we did not expect him to be that successful later."

During this period, there was another effort by Li that is worth noting. Hong Kong was a British colony, and English was widely spoken. If one's English was not good, it was difficult for him to achieve much. Li Ka-shing realized this, so he never stopped learning English.

He wrote down English words on cards. He would take them out in the teahouse or at the watch company, wherever and whenever he had time, glance at them and repeat the words. Gradually, he was able to communicate with his cousin in simple English, which surprised Chong Yuet Ming. She was in awe of her cousin's gift of intelligence and came to have a crush on him.

As the work was not very pressing in the watch company, Li Ka-shing had more spare time. He secretly resolved to make use of his free time to learn middle school courses. However, there was a problem – where to get the textbooks? Buying from a bookshop was the simplest and most direct way, but with his meagre salary, and his younger brother's and sister's tuition to pay for, he had little money left.

Li realized that many middle school graduates in Hong Kong sold their used textbooks to waste stations. So, he was able to buy them for the price of waste paper. After reading and studying, he sold them again as waste. He achieved his goal of learning, and in the long run he did not spend a penny. This was his little trick, and another sign of his intelligence. Many years later, when he reflected on this matter, it still delighted him: "Indeed, I gained knowledge and saved money, killing two birds with one stone."

In fact, he was happy not because of the money saved, but because, in the process of buying and selling, he found pleasure in doing business.

In 1946, a year after Japan's surrender, Hong Kong was on the right track. The population increased to more than one million again, the economy was recovering rapidly, and everything seemed to be full of vitality. As an outstanding Teochew businessman, Chong Ching On keenly felt all this and wanted to expand the watch company again. He wanted to build a new factory and have his own brand. He also wanted to venture into Southeast Asia.

He harboured great ambition and had big plans for the development of his company. However, he had not expected Li Ka-shing to share his ambition. Li looked up to him, paid attention to what his uncle did and tried to learn from him, and ambition can be infectious. Perhaps Uncle Chong did not know it yet, but Li Ka-shing was already full of ambition.

If Li had stayed at the watch company, he could have developed with the business and, with hard work and his uncle's help, perhaps one day he could own it himself. But Li Ka-shing felt that he should give it all up. Why? Because he wanted to carve out his own future, in his own industry, and be independent.

Therefore, to everyone's surprise, Li Ka-shing submitted his resignation.

But he had several people to persuade. The first was his mother, who firmly opposed his resignation. She saw the bright prospects of her brother's company and her son's future in the enterprise. But Li Ka-shing's words made her speechless. He declared that he wanted to have his own factory before the age of 24. At that time, he was not even 18 years old. But time waits for no man; he was convinced that he had to move forwards more independently.

Chong Bik Kam did not expect her son to be so ambitious. She could do nothing but give her consent. But how could he explain this to Uncle Chong? In times of difficulty, it was his uncle who always gave a helping hand. And at the moment, the fast-growing company needed as much talent as it could get.

Li Ka-shing took another approach. He wanted to work as a salesman in a hardware factory. So, he asked the factory boss to go to Chong Ching On for a salesperson.

"Relieving the state of Zhao by besieging the state of Wei," Chong Ching On said of his nephew's scheme, and he decided to talk to him personally.

After a long talk between the uncle and the nephew, Chong Ching On understood young Li's ambition. His heart was not shocked, but touched, for he didn't expect that his sister would have such a promising son. Finally, Chong Ching On sighed, "All right, it might be the best for you to see the bigger world."

4. THE GREAT SALESMAN

Og Mandino, an American writer of inspirational and self-help books, published *The Greatest Salesman in the World* in 1968. Mandino thought that selling was both an art and a science. "Selling is to let others know, like and trust the salesman," he wrote. "When you communicate with others sincerely, you have already taken a successful first step to sell yourself."

Li Ka-shing had accumulated a rich knowledge of how to judge people, and a sincere and diligent attitude towards work. He was soon selling galvanized white iron buckets for the hardware factory. Instead of looking for retail shops, he took his wares directly to restaurants, hotels and housewives in residential areas.

As Mandino said, selling is to make friends and let others like you. Li Ka-shing seemed to have figured this principle out for himself. When the owner of a hotel refused his bucket, he did not give up. He found out that the owner's child liked collecting stamps, so he managed to get a set of rare stamps and gave them to the man. In one fell swoop, he closed the distance between himself and the owner, and they became friends.

And with that, the hotel agreed to purchase 200 buckets at once, giving Li a big deal.

Fearing no trouble, he walked directly into residential areas. When he saw groups of older residents, he would step forwards and introduce his product. He knew that as long as one of these people made a purchase, it would become an advertisement and would bring more customers. So, he went to great lengths to explain and even demonstrate the advantages and durability of his buckets.

At that time, Li Ka-shing was often seen carrying a large bag and samples, taking buses, crossing roads and rushing from one place to another. Hardworking, simple, earnest and sincere, he moved many of those who came into contact with him. They supported Li, and his sales far exceeded those of his counterparts.

But he lost one deal in particular, and this became a turning point in his life.

At a large hotel, the boss had promised to buy his iron buckets. However, before signing the agreement, a middle-aged man walked in with a plastic bucket. Without many words, the other salesman demonstrated the advantages of his product. In comparison, the plastic bucket was obviously superior to the iron one.

The boss renounced his verbal agreement with Li Ka-shing on the spot and ordered the plastic buckets instead.

As Li Ka-shing was leaving, the salesman stopped him and invited him to a tavern. They drank and talked. It turned out that the man was the boss of a plastic factory. "Plastics is a new industry, while the galvanized bucket business is already on the decline," he told Li. "There is nothing wrong with your marketing strategy. It is your product that failed you. Why don't you come and work with me? I need a guy like you."

Li Ka-shing was stunned by the man's words. The first thing to do in business is to choose the right industry. Plastics was, in the late 1940s, like a rising sun on the horizon, offering great potential. He accepted the man's invitation and immediately went to work for the plastic factory.

After making the move, he continued to act as usual – taking buses, running across roads and rushing from one place to another with a big backpack on his back. The plastic factory was located in a remote area. To get there, Li sometimes even took a ferry across Victoria Harbour. But he never complained, for he believed that complaining was for people who had no ambition. He voluntarily worked 16 hours a day and ran around every corner of Hong Kong to sell.

Once, he came to a wholesale shop when the clerk was cleaning up. He decided to do a demonstration on the spot. He immediately took out his plastic sprinklers, which were an entirely new type of product. It was necessary to explain its functionality, but to see it in operation spoke louder than anything. The manager saw how well the gadget worked and immediately signed a deal. This taught Li Ka-shing that actions speak louder than words.

Li's sales promotion relied not so much on words as on his enthusiastic attitude, meticulousness in work and honesty. If he had a 10am appointment, he would never arrive at 10.01. The promises he made to his friends would always be delivered on, regardless of the difficulties. He did not talk much, but everything he did lived up to others' expectations. This made people feel that he was honest and reliable, and that they could get along with him. As a result, he made a lot of friends.

Know the rules, observe them and honour the contracts – this was his motto and the principle he treasured in his heart. He didn't take shortcuts. He didn't believe in the 'Thirty-Six Stratagems' in *The Art of War*, which he believed was the dross of Chinese culture, because it taught people to achieve their goals unscrupulously.

Of course, he also had many specific strategies. He paid great attention to the market situation and market information collection. He divided Hong Kong into several regions and recorded the population and consumption capacity of each region in his sales notes. He also subscribed to many industry magazines to keep abreast of international plastic products and market trends.

Li Ka-shing's endeavor paid off. In the year-end appraisal, his sales performance was the best in the company. It was, in fact, seven times higher than the second-best seller's. What a remarkable salesman!

At the age of 18, he became the project manager of the plastic factory. The next year, he became the factory's general manager. His new position brought about new challenges. While he could read people's faces, repair clocks and promote sales, but he did not know much about management and factory production. So, he wore his work clothes every day and delved deep into the workshop.

He learned carefully from skilled workers and tried everything himself. Finally, he learned all of the procedures of plastic production and understood how to manage workers. He became the head of the factory, with a commanding knowledge of sales, production and management.

From an ordinary teahouse boy to the general manager of a plastic factory, such was his early rise. Not only did he understand interpersonal relations and how to deal with people, he also mastered many technologies associated with clocks and plastics. By this time, his salary was already considerable, as was the huge amount of commissions he made from his sales. Li Ka-shing could have had a good life if he continued this way, achieving a typical middle-class lifestyle.

But Li was naturally fond of challenges and liked to break barriers. He was never one to settle for the status quo. Despite his modest and steady appearance, he harboured great ambition, and his future was beyond anyone's imagination.

Li's boss at the plastic company had a keen eye for discerning talent, but he also had an open mind. At this critical moment, he found that Li Ka-shing could not be retained, so he hosted a farewell dinner for him. During the dinner, Li said, "I leave your company to set up a plastic factory myself. It is inevitable that I will use the technology I have learned from you and will probably develop some similar products. Now plastic factories are springing up everywhere. Even if I don't do it, others will do it anyway. However, I will not take away your customers or use your sales network to promote my products. I will open other sales lines."

This was Li Ka-shing, honest and straightforward.

In any case, at the age of 20 he had come to a turning point of his life – he was about to start his own business. As the saying goes: "Strong winds are blowing and clouds are tumbling!" At that moment, no one could possibly have known that Li would become the business tycoon who would so strongly influence Hong Kong's economy in the future. Indeed, Li himself did not know it yet.

Both slightly drunk as the farewell dinner came to a close, Li Ka-shing and the boss hugged each other goodbye. Goodbye, the once miserable boy! Goodbye, the teahouse, the watch shop, the hardware factory and the plastic factory. Actually, a plastic factory would remain part of the story, but this one would be Li Ka-shing's very own.

CHAPTER

THE KING OF PLASTIC FLOWERS

1. CHEUNG KONG PLASTIC FACTORY

On 1 May 1950, firecrackers were set off against a blue sky at Shau Kei Wan, a beautiful corner of Hong Kong. The sight was dazzling and the sound was deafening. A brand-new sign was hung on one side of an old gate, with the name 'Cheung Kong Plastic Factory,' glittering in the sun.

A young man in a suit and tie pressed his hand against his chest and looked at all this, with his eyes glowing. That young man was Li Ka-shing, and that factory was his factory. The name Cheung Kong – which means Yangtze River, running fast and far for tens of thousands of li, with great momentum – showed the young man's ambition.

When the fireworks stopped, he bent down to pick up a piece of brick near the door and threw it into the open space in the distance.

The factory was shabby and remote, situated in the far suburbs of Hong Kong. However, even a place like that had to be rented. Li had only HK$50,000, and he had equipment to purchase and workers to employ. That was Li Ka-shing at 20, young on the face but stern in the heart.

The young man, who was rather inarticulate, made a speech in front of many workers, probably for the first time. "Our factory is small, but I know the plastic industry better than most people," he said. "I believe that in the near future, our factory will become bigger and everyone will earn more money."

There was no applause; the workers looked at the slight, immature boss with questioning eyes.

But before long, the workers found that their boss was very hard-working. He got up at 4am every morning, washed himself, and immediately went to the street to promote or purchase what was needed. Except for the work on the factory's assembly line, Li took over all other managerial work. Calculating the time carefully, he would step into a client's office just as the person arrived at work. To save money, he never took a taxi; he either walked or took a bus. He tried hard to save every bit of time and money that he could.

By noon, Li Ka-shing would appear in the factory, as he would always check the work done that morning. Then, he would dine with the workers. The food was very simple, and there was no dining room or even a table. Most of them just sat on the floor or anywhere else they found convenient. Seeing the miserable condition of the workers, Li Ka-shing felt uneasy. He swore that the first money the factory made would be used on better meals for the workers.

Sure enough, soon after the factory became better off, the workers had their own canteen. Such was the attitude of Li Ka-shing, who had always said that "one must treat others with sincerity, and others will reciprocate." It was for this reason that, despite the backwards conditions of the factory, the workers all stayed loyal to Li and only few of them left the company.

At night, when all was silent, Li Ka-shing got even busier. He was the manager, accountant, cashier and designer. He would record the income and expenditures in an account book, design new products, and arrange the following day's work. He worked 16 hours a day, with a heavy workload.

The first products the factory turned out were plastic toys, which Li decided on after careful consideration and analysis of the market. Cheung Kong Plastic Factory had old equipment and lacked quality workers. Li Ka-shing was the only one who really knew the business of plastic production technology. Therefore, they were not in a position to produce higher quality plastic products. Plastic toys were very popular among children, and they were easy to make.

After careful planning, 50 plastic toy guns came off the assembly line. Li Ka-shing was happy when he saw the machines roaring and the plastic toys slowly rolling off the line.

With a wave of his hand, he took his employees to a nearby pub. Although the dishes were simple, they were sufficient. Li, who had always been thrifty, invited his workers to have a good drink to celebrate Cheung Kong Plastic Factory's first batch of products.

The products were well received, and the first batch sold out quickly. The market responded well to their quality and price, which greatly boosted Li Ka-shing's confidence. In addition to personally training workers and sharing technical guidance, he also expanded the sales team. He found several smart workers, taught them his own tips and methods of marketing, and personally led them to sell.

Orders came one after another. The roaring of the machines was even and steady. Li Ka-shing was intoxicated with the joy of success. But at that time, Shau Kei Wan was nothing more than a remote corner of Hong Kong. Among so many factories, Cheung Kong Plastic Factory was like a drop in the ocean. It was still small compared with other plastic factories.

But, in addition to his careful calculations and hard work, Li Ka-shing also took advantage of the social environment of the times to drive the success of his business.

It is fair to say that Cheung Kong Plastic Factory hitched a ride on Hong Kong's economic boom.

On 25 June 1950, the Korean War broke out. The British government ordered the closure of all trade routes to China, and Hong Kong's re-export trade plummeted instantly. Hong Kong, as the main export channel of the People's Republic of China, had lost its prime function. As a result, its economy, which was based on export trade, lost its direction.

In order to find their footing again, Hong Kong's governing authorities quickly adjusted their economic policies and changed the export trade approach to foster local manufacturing industries. A series of policies were issued, favorable to local manufacturers.

In recognition of local conditions, Hong Kong's government adopted an overseas sales strategy, relying heavily on the abundant local labour resources.

As plastic was a new industry, it had broad prospects. It also required less investment and could produce quick results, which was suitable for small and medium-sized investors. Aided by the supportive new economic policies, plastic manufacturing seemed to have grown wings. Many products were distributed beyond Hong Kong and were headed for southeast Asia, even finding markets in Europe and the United States.

As long as there were products, they would be sold out immediately. Therefore, orders came one after another, forming a virtuous circle. The profits were considerable, and they were rolled back into production.

Li Ka-shing recruited another batch of workers, and soon, yet another batch. He divided them into several groups and had experienced employees train them.

Sometimes, Li himself would teach the new recruits, working with them hand-in-hand. Now that he had enough workers, improving work efficiency became necessary. He divided production into three shifts, providing 24-hour-a-day coverage. Thus, the machines would never stop running, and the products would go down the assembly line uninterrupted.

Then he recruited accountants, cashiers, salesmen, purchasers and other managerial staff. The factory was becoming more and more standardized, and everything was on the right track.

Next, he rented a small attic in the San Po Kong district, installed a telephone, and turned the space into the factory office and product exhibition room. He had someone build a cubicle as his bedroom, and he lived there, integrating himself into the factory.

As things were now efficiently humming along, he sometimes went home to see his mother, brother and sister. His mother was always grateful to see her son, and she always urged Li to rest well and not to overstrain himself.

He would also go to his uncle's home to learn about managing enterprises. More importantly, his cousin Chong Yuet Ming was there, and seeing her would always bring a beam of sunshine to his heart. If he couldn't see her, Li Ka-shing would feel disappointed. As Chong Yuet Ming was in high school at Ying Wa Girls' School, the two were not able to see each other often. But every time Li saw his cousin, he felt that she had changed – her eyes seemed brighter, her skin fairer and her looks prettier.

Chong Yuet Ming was Li Ka-shing's Cantonese and English teacher, and the cousins were also childhood friends. Whenever Chong Yuet Ming met Li, she would always ask many questions, especially ones about the factory. Hearing that his struggle had borne fruit, Chong Yuet Ming was very happy. She always encouraged him and affectionately watched him leave.

But her father, Uncle Chong, always tried to send Chong Yuet Ming away at the time of Li's visits. This often left him feeling disappointed, as he managed to return home only once a week.

Having no other options, he could only suppress his feelings and devote himself to the management of the factory and the research and development of new products. Perhaps that was the only way.

However, due to his focus on expanding production, Li neglected one thing that almost brought about the end of Cheung Kong Plastic Factory.

2. HONESTY AND CREDIBILITY

There has never been a smooth path for the Yangtze River after it flows out of the glaciers.

After thousands of twists and turns, it plunges into high mountains and valleys, stirring up waves and rippling up the banks. Viewers turn pale at the sight of such a scene.

Was Li Ka-shing ready for the plunges, twists and turns that lay ahead? To be honest, no!

Smooth sailing will make anyone lose vigilance, let alone people in their early 20s. The factory was running at full capacity, and new employees were being recruited one batch after another. But with this came the problem of ageing equipment and unskilled workers. With the young boss full of pride, it was hard to avoid quality problems.

The general environment was also changing. Plastic factories had mushroomed all over Hong Kong, and new products came out every day. As a result, expectations and requirements were getting higher and higher.

Finally, one day, the mounting quality-control problems came into sharp focus when a middleman returned a batch of the factory's goods.

Li Ka-shing was shocked, but before he had time to think about the reason, goods started to flood back into the factory at the same rate they had once left it.

It was a familiar old story: in good times, everything goes smoothly, while in bad times, everything goes against you. Banks heard the news, and they not only stopped lending, but also forced Li to repay his debt immediately. Some raw material suppliers also seemed to have heard the news and came to demand payment for their supplies. As the saying goes: "Good news never leaves the house, but bad news travels thousands of miles."

The quality of Cheung Kong Plastic Factory's products was admittedly poor. When new clients visited the factory and saw the condition of the equipment, they would leave in a hubbub. This was a serious blow to the company's reputation.

Li Ka-shing was clearly unprepared for this overnight turn of events. He responded passively, first letting workers go and then treating merchants with rage as they returned goods. As a result, the families of the workers went to the factory to protest, and merchants shared news with each other, causing an overstock of all the plastic products.

It was a critical period. Perhaps it was time to shut down the factory. Some suggested to Li that he should simply sell the business so he could pay off his debt.

Li Ka-shing was heartbroken. Cheung Kong Plastic Factory was the result of his painstaking effort, and he expected its success to be as vast as the Yangtze River. He felt that there was something wrong with his business philosophy and method. When he returned home, his mother told him a story.

A long time ago, she said, there was an ancient temple in Sangbu Mountain outside Chaozhou City. The host, Monk Yun Ji, felt that he was dying and that there were not many days left for him. So, one day, he called his two disciples, Yi Ji and Er Ji, to him and handed them two bags of grain seeds. He told them to sow the seeds and come back in the harvest season. Whoever reaped the most grain could inherit his mantle and be the host of the temple. From then on, Monk Yun Ji closed his door to chant sutras and did not tend to the affairs of the temple. Soon, the harvest season came. Yi Ji carried a heavy load of millet to Yun Ji, but Er Ji went empty-handed. Yun Ji asked Er Ji why he was empty-handed. Er Ji honestly replied that he did not manage the field well and the seeds did not sprout. Unexpectedly, Yun Ji gave Er Ji his cassock and earthen bowl and asked him to be the host of the temple. Yi Ji was, of course, not satisfied. Yun Ji said calmly: "I guess you don't know that I had cooked all the seeds I had given you." Hearing this, Yi Ji was speechless, and left in disappointment.

This story made Li Ka-shing realize immediately that he was wrong. At this critical moment, he must not act too hastily and must treat people with sincerity. If he was wrong, then he should admit it, ask others for forgiveness and beg for a chance to undo the wrongdoing. This was the way out of the crisis.

Therefore, the first thing he did was to get things settled down at the factory. He held a general meeting, sincerely apologized to the workers and took all of the blame.

He admitted that his poor management had caused the problems. All the laid-off workers could come back to work as soon as the situation improved, he announced, and the factory would reissue their salaries.

He also said confidently that Cheung Kong Plastic Factory would get out of its current predicament. As long as there were high-quality products, the factory would not collapse. He would never sell the factory either. He hoped the whole staff would help him. The difficulties were only temporary, he assured them.

It was the first time that Li had made such a passionate speech. Seeing their young boss so confident and energetic, the workers were touched.

Then, he kept on visiting banks and suppliers, sincerely apologizing and admitting that he had mismanaged. If given some time, he insisted, he would turn things around.

His sincerity moved the bankers and suppliers, but the reprieve was limited. The bank promised to postpone collecting the loan, but it would not lend again until the previous loans were paid back. The suppliers also promised a grace period but would not supply more material until things were set straight.

Li Ka-shing did not push his luck. After buying more time, he immediately went to visit his customers. They were Cheung Kong Plastic Factory's lifeline. Without them, the business could not escape bankruptcy. These customers, who once had such a good relationship with the factory, mostly forgave Li Ka-shing.

One of the middlemen had once quarreled with Li Ka-shing about the quality of his products. Li came to his door and sincerely said, "I blame myself for our quality problem in the past. I was wrong!" The man was not expecting that Li's attitude would change so much, and he also forgave him.

After stabilizing banks, suppliers and customers, Li Ka-shing began to sort out the products. These were the root cause of the problem; he found that some of the products were defective, and some were returned by middlemen due to delays and misinformation. Then, he carefully tested all the products and weeded out the faulty ones.

Next, he began to direct his energy back towards the market, and personally promoting his wares. The quality-assured products were sold as usual while the defective ones were marked as inferior and sold at a lower price. In this way, his products were gradually accepted again by the market and the situation gradually improved.

This time, Li Ka-shing kept things steady. First, he paid back the debt to suppliers to ensure that the factory could run smoothly. In this process, he recruited previously laid-off skilled workers, and picked some flexible-minded employees to do sales, so they could clear up the backlog of goods. They stuck to the policy of honesty and reliability and clearly labeled good products and lower-quality ones.

The factory slowly restored its credibility, and the negative news about Cheung Kong Plastic Factory disappeared bit by bit.

The bank could see that the factory was now in good operating order. They were very happy to lend to Li again, especially after he'd paid back all the previous loans.

This seemed to happen over a relatively short time, but in fact, it was a long haul. Step by step, the factory recovered, and Li Ka-shing found his anchor again. It was quite a struggle, but Li made it.

One day in 1955, four years after the crisis, Li called a general meeting. He first bowed three times to his employees, thanking them for their cooperation in difficult times and for their constant support.

"Our factory has basically paid off its debts," he told them. "Yesterday, we were informed by the banks that from now on, we can receive new loans. This shows that our factory has shaken off the crisis and has entered a brand new era."

Li Ka-shing stepped down from the podium and gave each worker a red envelope containing a bonus. Each of them took a moment to hold Li Ka-shing's hands tightly. Everyone knew how hard this young man had been working, and that it was not an easy thing. No one needed to utter a single word; a firm handshake spoke for everyone.

With the joint effort of both the labour force and the capitalists, Cheung Kong Plastic Factory had finally weathered the crisis and come to life again.

It was late at night and there were stars in the sky. Li Ka-shing climbed up the hillside behind the factory. In front of him was the brightly lit Victoria Harbour. The lights were reflected in the seawater.

Sitting on a cold stone, his thoughts wandered. Scenes of the past four years flashed in his mind and seemed increasingly vague and distant. He could not deny that Cheung Kong Plastic Factory was like a ship, and he was inarguably the captain, which left him no room to be rash and sloppy. He must steer carefully, see the route clearly and avoid hidden rocks and shoals.

In a moment of clarity, he resolved to development in stability, and not forget stability while developing.

Being prosperous for the first year and struggling in hardship for the next four gave Li Ka-shing many thoughts.

He knew that the factory was still crossing through ravines and it was not yet capable of making waves for thousands of li to come.

However, the ups and downs of the past few years had taught him a lifelong lesson. He concluded that capital was the blood of an enterprise and the source of its life, and credibility was the backbone of an enterprise. For young Li Ka-shing, and the young Cheung Kong Factory, this lesson was a bountiful reward earned through hardship.

3. A TRIP TO ITALY

Seen from the air, Italy lies like a boot in the vast blue Mediterranean Sea. The heel of the boot teeters above Africa and the boot's barrel is tucked into Europe. Therefore, she is like a bridge connecting Africa and Europe.

Carrying the glory of the ancient Roman Empire, the Renaissance awakened Europe and gave a new life to this ancient continent, from which modern Western civilization was born. Six hundred years ago, Marco Polo started here on his trip to China along the Silk Road, becoming a household name among the Chinese people.

Six hundred years later, in 1957, Li Ka-shing landed in Rome. What did he want to do there?

Although Cheung Kong Plastic Factory survived the crisis, it had a tremendous impact on Li Ka-shing. He could not help thinking: with so many plastic factories in Hong Kong, what can we rely on to survive and compete well into the future? After thinking for a long time, he came to the conclusion that it was the development of new products. Developing new products could not only rejuvenate the factory, but also bring novelty to the market and make consumers appreciate and buy your products for a pleasant change of pace.

Only in this way, he realized, could the factory survive, grow and move forwards like the Yangtze River.

One day, by chance, he saw in a magazine that Italy produced plastic flowers that sold well all over Europe.

Many people may have seen the magazine, but Li Ka-shing was the only one who was inspired by it. He immediately realized that plastic flowers were fantastic new products, and they would lead to a new trend in the Chinese plastic industry. Perhaps this is the kind of consciousness that allows somebody to become an influential entrepreneur.

And so, Li went to Rome for plastic flowers.

Rome has gone through many vicissitudes, leaving behind the glory of the great empire. But Italians are not only romantic, they are also good craftsmen. Their leather goods are beautiful and durable; their glass is colorful; their Ferraris and Lamborghinis are the world's top sports cars. The plastic flower is but a small player among all of those innovations, but it stirred the heart of a Chinese youth and made him travel all the way to Rome.

Thanks to his cousin's efforts over the years, Li Ka-shing's English had reached a certain level, and there was no problem for him to communicate with the Italians in that international language of business.

After two days of hard work, he found a manufacturer of plastic flowers. He first tidied himself up, dressed in a suit, tie and polished shoes. Entering the factory, he introduced himself as a plastic flower distributor from Hong Kong who wished to sell the company's products in Hong Kong. This made the Italian factory manager very happy, as he was in charge of sales. It was an irresistible temptation for any European manufacturer to open up a new market in the Far East. Besides, the young man was very polite and sincere.

The manager showed Li Ka-shing into the product exhibition room, where all kinds of plastic flowers blossomed like real ones. Li secretly marveled at how ingenious humans could be, competing with nature in creating beauty. If you didn't touch these flowers with your own hands, you couldn't tell whether they were real living things or not.

Li Ka-shing was, after all, himself. He was not intoxicated with the beauty of plastic flowers, nor had he forgotten his identity. He picked up a bundle of flowers and commented on them. Because of his familiarity with the plastic industry, what he said was absolutely expert. Hearing this, the other manager did not dare to cold-shoulder him, and immediately gave him an all-round explanation.

And with that 'inside' information, Li fully had a clear picture of the production process.

He would pick up a bouquet of roses and critique them, prompting the manager who would justify the product and take the chance to boast about it. Then, Li would put down the roses, pick up a lily and offer his critical observations. After round after round of this, he packed up samples of each kind of flower and paid for them.

The Italian manager was happy, feeling that his hard day's work had finally paid off. He warmly saw Li Ka-shing to the door, telling him that their plastic flowers were the best in Italy, and that long-term cooperation would definitely bring Li a lot of profits. The two said goodbye with a hug.

In the evening, facing a room full of plastic flowers, Li Ka-shing was bewildered. Why? Although he now understood how to produce plastic flowers, he was still vague about the toning formula and other fine points, which were of crucial importance. Without the detailed specifics, he would not be able to produce perfect plastic flowers.

Reflecting on the the crisis his business had faced, after he had let product quality slip, Li Ka-shing dared not take things lightly ever again. He was determined that he would not return to Hong Kong without the coloration formula and a real understanding of the entire fabrication process.

Perhaps the saying that, "heaven never seals off all the exits" is right, and the Bible also says, "When God has closed a door for you, he will surely open a window for you somewhere else."

The next day, Li Ka-shing stumbled upon an advertisement for an Italian plastic factory that was recruiting workers. A flash of light went through his mind: "Isn't this my chance?"

This plastic factory was a branch of the previous one, and it was located some distance away. Therefore, Li was not afraid that he would bump into the sales manager with whom he'd dealt. He changed into some shabby clothes and went to the branch.

His tourist visa did not allow him to work in Italy, but the business could offer a desperate immigrant without the right visa just half of the normal salary. Sure enough, the greedy manager offered Li a job.

And so, Li Ka-shing became a Chinese worker in an Italian plastic factory that specialized in realistic artificial flowers.

He was as diligent as ever, and as a lowly helper he always knew what the master worker wanted as soon as he raised his hand. Li would hand him the things he needed quickly. The work assigned to him was to remove waste, which was advantageous. He could push the cart around in various workshops. He would keep a close eye on the equipment and watch how workers mixed the ingredients and operated the machines. Due to his deep understanding of the plastic industry and his intelligence, he soon had a primary mastery of the toning formula.

Of course, the accuracy of what he had ascertained could not be verified. Therefore, he would treat the skilled workers every weekend in a tavern. After pouring everyone a cup of brandy, Li Ka-shing asked sincerely: "Please teach me. I can't be a worker who removes waste forever. I have a family to support."

Brandy is bright in color, soft at the first sip, but has a powerful and long-lasting effect. When these skilled masters had become drunk enough, they told Li everything he needed.

It would not be hard to guess that Li Ka-shing would be a fast learner. Soon after, Li was confident that he had learned all the production processes, toning formula and other specific techniques of plastic flower production. So, he went to the store again, bought plastic flowers of every variety, packed them in boxes and sent them to the airport, where he too boarded a plane back home.

As he buckled his seat belt, the crisp sound was so pleasant that Li Ka-shing lay back as far as possible and stretched out his body. At that moment, he was no different from all the other passengers on the plane. But how could anyone know that this young man was about to be extraordinarily famous in Hong Kong?

The plane took off. Through the window, Li Ka-shing could see the floating clouds under the wing and the increasingly distant blue sea.

Goodbye, Italy, and goodbye, Mediterranean Sea!

4. THE EVERLASTING FLOWERS OF HONG KONG

In the conference room of Cheung Kong Plastic Factory, the key managers and technicians were all attracted by the plastic flowers Li had laid out. They spoke about them enthusiastically, whispering to each other, admiring their vividness and feeling that their boss must be launching a new plan.

As expected, Li Ka-shing, calm as he had always been, waited until the discussion abated and then announced his decision: from that moment on, the main products of Cheung Kong Plastic Factory would be plastic flowers. All personnel were to realize this, embrace it and work hard on the production and sale of the new products.

Without delay, Li recruited a large number of talent in plastics to develop plastic flowers suitable for the Hong Kong market.

Plastic flowers are, of course, copies of genuine flowers, and different places have different preferences. For instance, Italians like tulips. After careful surveys, Li found that the people of Hong Kong liked hydrangeas the best. He asked his technicians to do more work on the toning formula, molding combinations and style variety. They should adapt to the market and ensure quality. Previous mistakes must be avoided. Quality was of the utmost importance if the new venture was to succeed.

The first thing they made were wax samples. Li Ka-shing personally took these samples to the market and listened carefully to feedback. After more than a month of trial and error, the first batch finally rolled off the assembly line.

When this batch of plastic flowers entered the market, many dealers were shocked. An old customer couldn't help asking: "Is this the product of your factory?"

Li Ka-shing smiled and responded with a teasing question of his own: "Or maybe I brought it back from Italy."

Indeed, these products were slightly different from the plastic flowers made in Italy, especially the local favorite varieties. As for questions about whether he had really produced them, Li said, "Although Cheung Kong Plastic Factory has shabby buildings, the equipment is new, and so are our staff and our business."

At that time, plastic flowers in the Hong Kong market were mostly imported from Italy. After going through all those hands in the process, they became very expensive and were seen as high-grade goods that only some British and Chinese white-collar workers could afford. But Li Ka-shing knew that the cost of mass produced plastic flowers was not high. Before long, they would bloom all over Hong Kong.

In order to seize the market first and gain credibility, he wanted to take the route of small profits but quick turnover. So, his price was almost half that of the current market rate.

As a result, the flowers sold out immediately. Some dealers even offered to prepay half of cost to obtain guaranteed delivery. Such good sales prospects breathed new life into Cheung Kong Plastic Factory. It produced large quantities of plastic flowers, and their sales expanded from Hong Kong to Southeast Asia.

The factory's machines roared incessantly, day and night. Staff worked in shifts, and the facilities were brightly lit around the clock. More varieties of plastic flowers, fruits and trees were developed, and rapidly taken to market. This was all Li Ka-shing's brainchild, because he understood that the production of plastic flowers was not complicated.

Given the large number of plastic factories in Hong Kong, more factories would imitate his work. Sure enough, soon afterwards, many manufacturers switched to producing plastic flowers. However, most of the market share had already been seized by Cheung Kong, and it was hard for the latecomers to compete. Li Ka-shing had anticipated this and had taken pre-emptive moves to head them off.

However, Li was not satisfied. The trip to Italy not only enabled him to acquire the technology to produce plastic flowers, but it showed him how Western capital worked, which shocked him greatly. If the business was to be bigger and stronger, only one Cheung Kong Plastic Factory would not be enough. The business had to grow.

At the end of the year, he changed the name of his business to Cheung Kong Industries. Its incorporation model was from the West. Being a corporation meant that it was a joint venture of a number of partners. Li Ka-shing began to solicit shares among his relatives and friends, and from that day on he envisaged something much greater that involved real estate and a stock exchange listing. Perhaps that was why he changed the name.

At the same time, he relocated the company to North Point, which is closer to the city. The organizational structure was more efficient, and a large company with modern management systems emerged.

Sales of the plastic flowers were in full swing, and they appeared in most of the markets in Hong Kong and Southeast Asia. But Li was not satisfied. He sought to press onward into Europe and North America.

The first target was Europe, but the European market was under the control of British firms. Any goods sold from Hong Kong to Europe had to pass through foreign firms, and they profited from that. Foreign firms simply could not be circumvented.

Li Ka-shing did not want foreign firms to profit from his business, and he did not want to be controlled by them or let them manipulate prices, which would damage the reputation of the company. He hoped that he could have direct access to European merchants.

So, he sent a troop of salesmen to Europe to directly contact wholesalers there. Of course, the wholesalers liked seeing their producers directly, and they hit it off. Cheung Kong Industries' plastic flowers were of good quality and low price, so they soon opened up the European market. Orders came in one after another, like falling snowflakes.

Unfortunately, the manufacturing operation was short of funds and the bank would not extend large-scale loans. Li Ka-shing therefore did not dare to take large orders, which upset him. He tried every means imaginable to break through the bottleneck.

Just when Li was feeling most helpless, a major European wholesaler came to him on his own initiative.

"Your plastic flowers are abundant in variety, good in quality and low in price, and are better than the Italian ones," the man told him. "I want to cooperate with you."

What would this involve? Li Ka-shing certainly understood that the wholesaler was not interested in simply purchasing his products; he wanted to underwrite their production. In this kind of model, dealers would invest a certain amount of money, which was exactly what Li Ka-shing yearned for. It would be the impetus for the nascent Cheung Kong Industries to develop further.

In any case, he could not miss this opportunity. He was full of hope and stared at the wholesaler, waiting for him to continue. As expected, the man said, "I can prepay some of the deposit, but you have to find a guarantor." This was reasonable enough; as he and the wholesaler were not familiar with each other, it made sense for Li Ka-Shing to have to have a guarantor. And so, he agreed.

However, in snobbish Hong Kong, no one would extend such a large-scale capital guarantee on mere conjecture and promises.

And so, literally overnight, Li Ka-shing produced nine types of samples in three batches, and went to see the wholesaler the next day. He placed the samples on the table, and the wholesaler was clearly shocked. He had asked for only three samples and did not expect that Li would reproduce each sample into three smaller varieties.

One group were flowers, another fruits and the other vegetation. The wholesaler took a string of purple grapes, scrutinized it closely, and it was apparent that he liked what he saw.

Finally, the wholesaler looked up at Li Ka-shing, whose eyes were bloodshot from a long night of labour, and smiled. "Mr Li, your nine samples are the best plastic products I have ever seen," he exclaimed. "We can talk about our cooperation now."

Li Ka-shing spread out his hands, abashed. "I'm sorry, I can't find a guarantor," he apologized, "but you know how eager I am to cooperate with you."

The man looked at him for a long time, and then suddenly raised his hand and said: "Well, I have found a guarantor for you."

Li Ka-shing was shocked. Was it possible? He was at a loss for words, but the wholesaler continued: "This guarantor is you. Your sincerity and credibility are the best guarantees."

Then, the wholesaler snapped his fingers and called up the hotel waiter. "Two glasses of champagne, please!"

On that day, Li Ka-shing felt that his chest was in full bloom with flowers. He drank up the champagne and felt wonderful. To the wholesaler who had come all the way from Europe, Li was deeply grateful.

With the investment from the wholesaler, Cheung Kong Industries expanded rapidly, the plastic flowers it produced went across the sea, and they had a major presence in the European market. In 1958, Cheung Kong Industries' turnover exceeded $HK10 million, and its profit hit HK$1 million. Li Ka-shing was 30 years old.

Then, as its plastics business grew, Cheung Kong Industries launched a new real estate business. Li Ka-shing leveraged his position as 'The King of Plastic Flowers' to expand into the property space.

However, the story of plastic flowers was not complete. There was still a sales territory Li aimed to conquer – North America. His plastic flower brochures and samples had already been sent there and had prompted some initial responses. A very large dealer wrote back asking for a field visit to Hong Kong. Li Ka-shing immediately replied: "Welcome to Hong Kong!"

Li also did a little research. It turned out that the company that had contacted him was very powerful and controlled the sales markets in Canada and the United States. What a once-in-a-lifetime event. But Li Ka-shing understood that they probably wouldn't just visit his company on their survey trip to Hong Kong. They must be planning to assess several other companies as well, and choose the best one.

There was no time for him to delay. He must show the best of his factory and have the inspectors choose it at first sight. But he had only seven days to make the necessary preparations.

Li returned the already obsolete factory building and found a standard factory building of more than 10,000 square metres in North Point. Then he purchased, installed and debugged the equipment. Time was so limited that he did not have the luxury of resting. For seven days and nights, Li Ka-shing and his workers carried out this seemingly impossible task.

Seven days later, all the machines in the new factory building were put into operation, and just as Li wiped the sweat from his brow and glanced at his watch, someone tod him he had a phone call. The North American dealers had arrived.

Li Ka-shing did not hesitate and drove a car in person directly to Kai Tak Airport. Upon receiving the visitors, Li asked, "Would you like to go to the hotel to rest first, or go to the factory?" He had anticipated the answer: "To the factory."

After entering the factory, the guests carefully inspected the workshop and the sample room. Li Ka-shing, who closely followed, found that the newly installed equipment was already being put into use; it was running well and everything was in good order.

He was happy deep within but put forwards a cool appearance, and calmly said, "Don't make yourself too tired. Tomorrow I will show you other plastic factories in Hong Kong."

The lead guest waved his hand and spoke in broken Chinese: "There is no need to see other factories. Yours is large, advanced, well organized and has far exceeded my expectations. I'm not flattering you – your factory can rival those in North America. It is even better than them."

Li Ka-shing suppressed his joy. "Rest assured, we will guarantee delivery time and quality," he said. "This is the core value and lifeline of our company."

The dealer burst out laughing: "Well, tomorrow we will sign the contract, and you are our sole supplier."

Cheung Kong Industries' plastic products entered the North American market, bringing in million-dollar orders every year. In addition, Li Ka-shing won the favor of the Canadian Imperial Bank of Commerce and was extended a line of credit. That laid a good foundation for him to bring more businesses to overseas markets.

Soon, Li completed the 12-storey industrial building in North Point, and Cheung Kong Industries had its grand headquarters.

In those years, it was reported that Hong Kong accounted for 80% of the plastic flower trade, making it the world's largest supplier. Besides the United States, more and more products were going to Japan, West Germany and Australia as well. Cheung Kong Industries became the world's top plastic flower manufacturer, and Li Ka-shing became the world-famous 'King of Plastic Flowers.'

CHAPTER

ENTERING THE REAL ESTATE BUSINESS

1. HONG KONG'S 'KING OF LAND'

North Point, as its name implies, is the northeast corner of Hong Kong. It faces Victoria Harbour and features large docks, where the Hong Kong Customs Building is situated. Most of the residents there are from the southeastern Chinese provence of Fujian, giving it the nickname 'Little Fujian.' Cheung Kong Industries' first office building was completed there in 1958. Soon, the second building was capped nearby in Chai Wan.

The completion and operation of these two structures had given Li Ka-shing a taste of the enormous potential of the real estate business. In addition to setting up offices for his own factory, the remaining space in the two buildings was rented out. He collected rental fees and property management fees, bringing in a steady flow of capital. In this way, his thoughts on real estate gradually took shape.

At that time, Hong Kong was rapidly expanding, its population going from 600,000 after the war to over 1 million and then to 2 million. Now, it was home to more than 3 million people.

The sharp increase in population resulted in a housing shortage. Hong Kong's government adopted a policy of high land prices, making property there extremely expensive. As a result, the real estate industry attracted many speculators. They used bank loans and sales of uncompleted flats, among other means, to rapidly build large numbers of buildings.

Li Ka-shing still adhered to the strategy of 'seeking development in stability.' He never sold uncompleted flats or used large bank loans. Only rental properties were developed, and the business was proceeding steadily, in line with his capabilities.

Some derided him for being overly conservative, and some said that he did not understand the double benefits brought by presale – that is, 'kidnapping' the bank, locking up the users and ensuring an inflow of capital. Li Ka-shing laughed this all off and went on with his rental business.

From 1959 to 1980, land prices in Hong Kong increased by 280 times. Developers who were eager to do presales sold every piece of land they had. So, when land prices rose, they did not have any buildings left. However, Li Ka-shing had been renting out his properties, so although the progress was slow at the beginning, in the long run it helped him keep lots of properties in hand. Thus, one can imagine the profits brought by the land price rise.

As a result, Li became Hong Kong's 'King of Land.' All the property he owned was like gold that increased in value by the day.

Amid turmoil in the real estate market, many developers went broke under the pressure of bank runs by clients. It is worth mentioning that Liu Po Shan, chairman of LCHB, died of a cerebral hemorrhage after being squeezed by clients due to real estate fluctuations. After that, Mingde Bank and Guangdong Trust Commercial Bank were affected by this as well. The banking industry in Hong Kong was even dragged into the crisis and the real estate industry plummeted.

Li Ka-shing was the only one who had kept the land, and his reputation, intact and in steady development.

Hong Kong's economy was hit like never before, triggering the 'Fleeing from Hong Kong' phenomenon. Many rich people emigrated overseas. Rumors of impending doom were circulating, causing panic.

Large numbers of buildings were left unfinished, and many of those completed were underselling. An independent foreign-style house with a garden at Stubbs Road Centre, the heart of Hong Kong, was sold for only HK$600,000. From that, one can imagine how far Hong Kong's real estate industry had plummeted.

Of course, Li Ka-shing was also at the centre of the storm. He tried his best to calm himself, reading newspapers and listening to the news every day, and carefully studying the situation.

At that time, the newspaper *Ming Pao* reported the 'Fleeing from Hong Kong' turmoil as follows:

"People were burning buses and trams, killing police, beating bus and tram drivers, burning Betty's Health, bombing postal services, bombing the Tai Po Rural Affairs Bureau, attacking teahouses, throwing stones at pedestrians and cars, firing fish cannons at the police, exploding water pipes, burning newspaper vehicles ..."

Li Ka-shing was worried, but he soon learned that the agitation against mainland China had gradually subsided in August and September. He believed that the so-called 'Fleeing' would not last long. The stability of Hong Kong was not only the wish of Hong Kong's people, but also the hope of mainland China's government.

He decided to buy property that others were underselling, acquiring it at its lowest price. Cheung Kong Industries bought huge numbers of property, rapidly expanding its holdings from 10,080 square metres to 30,150,000 square metres.

No one was optimistic about Li Ka-shing's actions. His friends warned him, and his foes just waited to see him fail. Li did not explain anything, laughing off the criticism.

Soon, President Deng Xiaoping made a high-profile announcement, calling on China to end the Cultural Revolution and focus on economic development.

All industries in Hong Kong were waiting to be revived, and real estate welcomed its upturn. At this point, Li Ka-shing had become the largest landowner in Hong Kong. His rental properties and land under construction were already priceless, and still gaining value.

A lot of people were dumbfounded. At the same time, they were a bit jealous, and some took to calling Li Ka-shing a 'casino magnate.' The meaning was clear – it had been nothing more than a big bet, and he had won.

In fact, how could those outsiders know how stormy Li Ka-shing's heart was when he was standing at the window of his office in North Point Industrial Building? Dark clouds once rolled over Victoria Harbour, and thunder and lightning once flashed over it. The bay was also hit by surges that could capsize ships at any moment.

His heart ached when profits from plastic flowers and income from rental properties went into real estate with no guaranteed future. He knew that if the People's Liberation Army wanted to occupy Hong Kong, they could do it in a minute.

But the reason it was not occupied in 1949 was that the Chinese government hoped to have a stable Hong Kong. "This hope still exists today," he said, "and Hong Kong will surely be stable." His judgment was full of wisdom, which many other people could not see. And that was why he had become Hong Kong's 'King of Land,' which nobody else had managed to do.

The greatest truths are the simplest. Such complicated business and investment behavior was actually as simple as that. This was not a big casino game, but it was the inevitable path of a winner in life. A gambler relies blindly on luck while a proven winner relies on knowledge, judgment and reason.

Such was Li Ka-shing. He did not drift along with others. He stood independently and used his judgment to win himself time and wealth.

Owners of capital are not the idle rich; they are full of wisdom. Every victory they win can be called classic and is backed by profound experience in, and time spent pondering, the ups and downs of life.

2. FIRST FRY

By then Cheung Kong Industries had changed its name to Cheung Kong (Holdings) Limited. It was like the Yangtze River reaching the mouth of the Three Gorges.

The first barrier in front of it was Hongkong Land, a large real estate company founded in 1889 by British businessmen Paul Chater and Jim Shaq, with a venture capital of HK$5 million. At that time, it was already one of the world's three largest real estate developers, with its officers referred to as 'real estate tycoons.' So, we can imagine how strong it was.

At a high-level meeting of Cheung Kong, Li Ka-shing said: "I believe everyone here knows about Hongkong Land, the Number 1 company in Hong Kong's real estate industry. We should learn from its success stories, find out our shortcomings, and let CK be as powerful as, or even more powerful than, Hongkong Land one day."

The attendees looked at each other in surprise and wondered, 'How will that be possible?'

However, the times produce their heroes. Just like Qutang Gorge, which is as robust as a tiger, Cheung Kong was beholden to no one else's will.

In the 1970s, the Hong Kong government decided to build subways. The subway company, Mass Transit Railway (MTR), was established, and the government adopted many preferential policies to ensure smooth construction.

The construction of properties on top of those subway stations attracted the attention of countless developers. These properties were all located in prosperous areas, meaning they could attract investment and be rented. They could bring huge business opportunities. The economic potential of every inch of the land was beyond estimation.

The Central MTR station and the Admiralty MTR Station are especially worth mentioning. Central is the head-end terminal of the system and is located in Hong Kong's banking area, its most prosperous region. Admiralty, close to Central, is linked to the banking area and is the transfer station for the East Extension and the starting point for the Cross-Harbour Tunnel. Hong Kong's government offices, the Supreme Court, the Red Cross and other office buildings are all nearby. If anyone was to develop property there, he would reap considerable profits.

The so-called real estate is, in effect, land. The position of the land determines the value of the property. If built in the wrong area, a building might be worthless. Although Cheung Kong had built its primary building in North Point, it had never set foot in Hong Kong's bustling downtown area. This was not just a defect; it was a great defect.

If Li wanted to up his game in the real estate industry, entering the downtown area would be the key.

Li Ka-shing had no other choice but to see marching into Central and Admiralty as his battle to victory. Meanwhile, Hongkong Land, with strength and abundant capital, had long regarded the Central and Admiralty subway stations as theirs.

It was to be a battle between a tiger and a cat. The winner seemed to be apparent before the battle even started. Indeed, they were all real estate developers, but the power gap between them was assumed to have determined the result.

In this battle, if Li Ka-shing won, he would settle in the central part of Hong Kong. If he lost, he would return to the suburbs. Li understood the importance of this campaign. One does not need the Thirty-Six Stratagems when dealing with other people. But in gearing up for a fight, the famous military directives were a perfect model to study.

The first thing Li had to do was to know the enemy and know himself. So, he gathered together all the information and studied up on his rivals and MTR.

MTR was a government-run company. However, apart from granting some special patents and concessions, the Hong Kong government had to carry out its funding, design, construction and operation in accordance with the laws of the market. In other words, if MTR wanted to auction the development rights for the two station superstructures, it could only do so under sound economic rules, not political rules. Simply put, even MTR would have to make money from the development of these two plots. That was the fundamental goal of the metro company.

Li Ka-shing also discovered that the Hong Kong government sold these two plots to MTR at over HK$200 million. MTR had discussed with local officials many times its desire to pay using some cash plus shares of MTR. However, the proposal was rejected by the government, which held to a resolute cash-only policy.

Cash was the biggest problem for MTR, for it had already run out of money. For this reason, the first piece of

Li Ka-shing's strategy was that the bidding must start with cash payment.

Second, Cheung Kong changed its long-held real estate strategy of renting only to selling only. That was also based on the actual situation of the subway company. MTR needed more money to invest in new subway construction. Renting out properties would not be able to bring in capital fast enough to carry out further construction. MTR would certainly not agree to a rental property model.

The third element of Cheung Kong's strategy was to surrender part of the profits. Li Ka-shing proposed that after deducting costs, the profits would be divided into 49% for CK and 51% for MTR.

After studying MTR, Li turned to his other rival, Hongkong Land. No matter how many other developers would bid, it was without a doubt Cheung Kong's biggest rival. This was due to its strength. It had been operating for many years in Hong Kong's central district. The Central MTR station was right across Chater Avenue, named after Paul Chater, co-founder of Hongkong Land. Across this avenue lay Chater Garden Square and at its left and right, the 'Land Plaza' and 'Recreation Plaza.' There were also dozens of Hongkong Land buildings standing nearby.

It was fair to say that the central district of Hong Kong was Hongkong Land's territory.

However, Li Ka-shing discovered a weakness in its organizational structure. That weakness was David Kennedy Newbigging, the Chairman of Hongkong Land, a Chinese who had served in the foreign firm for a long time. He had climbed to his position after decades of effort and was inevitably very meticulous.

The largest shareholder was Jim Keswick, whose development focus then was in overseas markets. This would surely distract Newbigging, making it difficult for him to devote himself fully to bidding for the Central and Admiralty station projects. A competition as fierce as this would be could not allow for any distraction. Unwavering focus was needed on every detail, because details determine success or failure.

Li Ka-shing believed that in terms of focusing on details, he already had an edge over the distracted Newbigging.

There were 30 real estate companies involved in the competition, all of which did their best. As soon as the battle started, gunpowder smoke filled the air. Various media had also smelled the news, and their coverage fanned the flames. In an interview with a well-known English reporter, Newbigging confidently stated: "The result of the bid is the final answer."

How confident he was. But the remark also implied his carelessness and arrogance. Perhaps he hadn't studied Li Ka-shing at all. He didn't seem to have paid any attention to 'little' Cheung Kong, off in its far corner of Hong Kong.

Of course, based on the situation at that time, he didn't need to pay any attention to Cheung Kong. Think about it. Surrounded by its own numerous roads, squares and buildings, how could the development of the two superstructures fall into the hands of others? Besides, Hongkong Land had a long history, and its strength far exceeded the sum total of the 30 companies.

And then, an unexpected piece of news set off a monstrous wave that made everyone turn pale.

On 5 April 1977, Hong Kong newspapers reported one after another on who would be granted development rights for the two superstructures. Among them, *The Industrial and Commercial Daily* reported that the right to develop the old post office property – the HK$240 million prime lot that was sought by 30 major consortia – was won by Cheung Kong (Holdings) Limited.

"According to the information from Mass Transit Railway, the conditions listed in the proposal submitted by Cheung Kong were exceptionally generous and attractive," the newspaper reported. "That was why they finally stood out and won exclusive development rights to the area, together with the Mass Transit Railway Corporation."

Before anyone could recover from the shock, MTR Chairman Tong Shun signed an agreement with Li Ka-shing on the development of the two superstructures and held a press conference.

"The building will be sold to the public floor by floor," Tong Shung told the crowd of reporters. "The benefits will be shared by CTR and Cheung Kong, with MTR taking the lion's share. A number of companies were interested in cooperating with us, so the competition was very fierce. After careful study, we chose Cheung Kong because their plan is the most attractive to us."

Jardine Matheson, Swire Group, Hutchison Whampoa Limited and Wheelock Properties were the four major foreign firms in Hong Kong. All told, they had held sway there for more than a hundred years.

Next, Li Ka-shing wanted to pocket the Kowloon Wharf. What did that mean? It signaled a march into the transportation, logistics and service industries after becoming big in the plastics and real estate sectors.

So, did Cheung Kong Holdings make it through the dangerous rapids of the Three Gorges?

CHAPTER 4

MONUMENTAL
EVENTS

1. HAVE A SENSE OF PROPRIETY AND MAKE DECISIONS PRUDENTLY

Li Ka-shing was attracted by an article by Zhou Zugui, a financial and economics critic from Hong Kong, entitled, "The Business of the Wharf Begins to Change." It said that if the Wharf Limited could take full advantage of its land resources, there would be positive momentum of 20% annual growth in the coming ten years.

It also predicted that the shares of the Wharf Limited, at the price of HK$13.50, would become a hot stock in 1978.

But the reality was that the Wharf had been issuing bonds continuously, with its shares slumping sharply. Li Ka-shing found that things depended on a big 'if.' The 20% annual growth would presumably come if the land resources were used to the fullest extent. However, the Wharf did not take good advantage of those resources. This was the conclusion of Li Ka-shing's study. So, if Li took control of the Wharf, he would make the best use of his land resources to achieve 20% annual growth.

Why didn't the Wharf make the most of its property? The group abided by a rental-only, not-for-sale land policy. Both Harbour City and Ocean Centre were famous buildings in Hong Kong. Then the Wharf moved freight service operations away to develop the land into commercial buildings.

All of this gradually exhausted its own funds. Its only-for-rent pattern slowed the return of the capital, leading to a financial crisis. It had to issue a large number of bonds to hedge cash with them. However, this was a vicious circle. With high debt, credit would inevitably decline and stocks would continue to fall.

How about Li Ka-shing? After the listing of his Cheung Kong Holdings, Li adopted a very flexible strategy on property rentals and sales. With plenty of money during the depressed housing market, he would rent out the property. If the property market went up and housing prices were high, he would speed up construction to promote sales, accelerating the return of funds.

Li Ka-shing was experienced and determined like this. The commercial world was like a battlefield where opportunities were uncertain and fleeting. So, he reasoned, one couldn't stick to the existing rules. Only those with flexibility could gain a decisive victory.

Therefore, Li conducted more in-depth studies on the Wharf. He calculated that at the end of 1977 and into early 1978, the price of the Wharf stock was between HK$13 and HK$14. The Wharf had issued less than 100 million shares, which implied that the total market value was less than HK$1.4 billion.

The Wharf was located in the 'golden section' of Kowloon, which should command between HK$6,000 and HK$7,000 per square foot at the official auction price. By that measure, its share price should be HK$50. If these plots could be properly developed, their value would skyrocket. So, even if Li bought the Wharf's stock at a price five times higher than the current one, it would still be impossible for him to lose money.

After the study and calculations were done, Li Ka-shing didn't hesitate – he bought 20 million shares right off the bat. What did that mean? It meant Li Ka-shing had a 20% stake in the Wharf.

The Wharf was a subsidiary of Jardine Matheson. In fact, there was a Hongkong Land property between them. Hongkong Land was an old rival of Cheung Kong Holdings. Li Ka-shing won a point in the battle for the over-track buildings. At the moment, Hongkong Land also held a 20% stake in the Wharf.

Of course, all of this had been done in silence. Unknowingly, the largest shareholder of the Wharf had changed, which not only surprised Hongkong Land, but also confused its parent company, Jardine Matheson.

However, since this was a 'war,' there would be no permanent win. Any hasty action might affect the ultimate direction of the 'battle.'

The stock market's abnormality and the sudden acquisition of the shares of the Wharf attracted many people's attention, especially the commentators who had been staring at the stock market day and night. Their endless commentary attracted many speculators, who put their money in.

By March 1978, the stock price of the Wharf had grown to HK$46 per share. At the same time, Li Ka-shing's way into the board of directors was not smooth. Under the rules of corporate governance, to get absolute control over a company, the shareholder must hold more than 50% of the shares. Otherwise, the acquired party would be able to mount a reverse takeover.

But now, Cheung Kong Holdings' share of the Wharf's stock had been bid up to 51%, which was by no means an advantage for Li Ka-shing. If he cut off all means of retreat, the risk would be so enormous that it could not be controlled, which Li absolutely didn't want to see.

At the same time, both Jardine Matheson and Hongkong Land took a cue from Cheung Kong Holdings' dynamism, mobilizing their funds to buy up shares of the Wharf from private investors. They had to increase their stake to a safe level and guard against Li Ka-shing's incursion. However, Jardine Matheson was no longer the powerhouse it had been. Its strength was declining, and could no longer match its ambition.

There was no way out. They had to appeal to HSBC for help, which shocked Michael Sandberg, the Executive Vice Chairman of the bank at that time.

Sandberg found Li Ka-shing. After they spoke, Li spent time deep in thought. The lights behind the window of No. 79 Deep Water Bay Road stayed on all night. It is impossible to know if his decision was made by himself or with the help of others. However, it was true that Li Ka-shing gave up the Wharf stock.

Afterwards, a series of events showed that Li's shrewdness was by no means comparable to that of the ordinary person.

It turned out that Sandberg had been entrusted by someone else: Pao Yue-Kong, a well-known Hong Kong shipping tycoon with whom he had a close personal relationship. Behind his powerful transport fleet stood HSBC. At the time, he also took a fancy to the Wharf. Of course, this was a shipping magnate's unique vision. The reasons behind it cannot be discussed here, but the conflict between his ideas and Li Ka-shing's was real.

If Li insisted on purchasing the stock, Sandberg would lose face and Li would be thrust into battle with Pao Yue-Kong. So, Li Ka-shing decided to step back.

In fact, most things in the world could be concluded with one of two moves, forwards or backwards. Most people don't consider the latter option, which is often more difficult to go through with. The hardest thing in the battlefield was not the hot pursuit to follow up the victory, but the retreat after a defeat. But Li Ka-shing retreated immediately, without any hesitation. His withdrawal left the Wharf to Pao Yue-Kong, and amounted to a favor to Sandberg.

In a book by Anna Pao Sohmen, *The World's Shipping Tycoon: Pao Yue-Kong's Biography*, there is this very vivid description:

"After a brief greeting, Li Ka-shing came straight to the point and expressed his willingness to transfer his 10 million shares of the Wharf to Pao Yue-Kong. Transfer? Pao Yue-Kong knew clearly that there was no penny from heaven. After a little reflection, he figured out Li Ka-shing's wisdom: Li Ka-shing knew Pao Yue-Kong very well and understood what he needed. Therefore, he used what Pao Yue-Kong needed in exchange for what he needed. This transfer would be beneficial to both of them."

From Pao Yue-Kong's point of view, with the 10 million shares of the Wharf from Li Ka-shing, together with his original shares, he became able to make a public bid with Jardine Matheson. If the acquisition succeeded, he could control the asset-rich Wharf.

From Li Ka-shing's point of view, he bought the shares for around HK$10 to HK$30, and now sold them to Pao Yue-Kong at more than HK$30, making tens of millions of Hong Kong dollars in a flash. More importantly, he could take over 90 million shares of Hutchison Whampoa from HSBC with Pao Yue-Kong's help. Once this goal was achieved, there would be no doubt that Li Ka-shing would become the Chairman of the Board of Hutchison Whampoa.

Such a brilliant idea could only have sprung from the mind of someone like Li Ka-shing. Pao Yue-Kong could not help secretly admiring this real estate upstart who was younger but clearly smarter than he was.

Without exclusive explanations, lengthy instructions or nagging bargaining, the two equally shrewd men chimed in easily and secretly concluded an equally prudent agreement.

Li Ka-shing sold the 10 million shares of the Wharf to Pao Yue-Kong for more than HK$300 million. Pao Yue-Kong assisted Li Ka-shing in acquiring over 90 million shares of Hutchison Whampoa from HSBC.

2. ACQUISITION OF HUTCHISON WHAMPOA

Hutchison Whampoa was a Western company. Its name reflected its two parts: Hutchison International, and Hong Kong and Whampoa Dock. At that time, Hutchison Whampoa was the second largest company owned by foreigners in Hong Kong and the largest listed company controlled by Hong Kong's top ten financial magnates.

Hutchison Whampoa was valued at HK$6.2 billion, while Cheung Kong Holdings, at best, was worth HK$693 million. In other words, Li Ka-shing's strength was only one-ninth of Hutchison's.

So why did Li Ka-shing back away from purchasing the Wharf, which was easy to take, and turn to Hutchison, which was so unattainable?

First, the Wharf was a family-owned enterprise that was highly unified. They would have fought the buyer to death. So, it was hard to say who could win the battle. Even if Li Ka-shing could achieve the final goal and become the owner of the Wharf, he would be scarred in the battle. As far as Cheung Kong Holdings was concerned, it might lose too much.

Later facts confirmed Li Ka-shing's judgment that Pao Yue-Kong had to pay HK$105 per share to become Chairman of the Board. Powerful as the shipping tycoon was, he only scraped through it, proving just how difficult the acquisition was.

Second, Hutchison Whampoa was superficially strong but, in fact, it had been disintegrated. It had already been partitioned by competing parties because of its poor management. Having been traded among multiple shareholders, it had already been turned from a family business into a joint venture. Among the stakeholders, the most important was HSBC.

In dealing with such enterprises, it would be difficult for the other side to form a joint force, making it easy to adopt strategies to attack them when they were unprepared and succeed in one stroke. HSBC controlled the vast majority of the shares, so to fix up HSBC basically meant to fix up Hutchison Whampoa.

Third, under commercial banking law, banks cannot engage in non-financial business. Creditor banks can accept equity in industrial and commercial enterprises that have lost the ability to repay their debts, but once a business is solvent and operating normally again, creditor banks must sell their stake to their original owners or other enterprises. So, sooner or later, HSBC would have to transfer the Hutchison Whampoa shares it controlled.

This was all on Li Ka-shing's mind. Pao Yue-Kong's sudden intervention made everything more fluid, and everything happened suddenly, but it all mapped to Li Ka-shing's expectations. That explains why Li suddenly changed his mind and quit the battle for the Wharf, in which he'd held a clear advantage.

In fact, Hutchison Whampoa was in the minds of all Chinese and foreign businessmen in Hong Kong. Everyone wanted this fat piece of meat. But considering that its biggest shareholder was HSBC, no one dared to mount a challenge, so they were still waiting.

At that time, the Chairman of Hutchison Whampoa was Edmond Wai Leung Ho, who had been a brain truster and senior counsellor but had never been in charge of a giant enterprise.

Following the company's poor management and excessive losses under previous leadership, things looked bleak, with little hope for a turnaround. The ownership structure had not been sorted out clearly, causing disagreements among shareholders. They were looking forwards to the appearance of an 'enlightened boss' who could turn back the power of darkness and help them emerge from the crisis.

All of this seemed to be waiting for Li Ka-shing. He appeared in the nick of time and marched resolutely into Hutchison Whampoa.

The relationship between Pao Yue-Kong and HSBC was beyond Li's influence, and he understood this. However, he handed over the shares of the Wharf respectfully. How could Pao Yue-Kong, who had never been in contact with him, not understand his meaning?

What kind of person was Pao Yue-Kong? When he took over Li Ka-shing's shares of the Wharf, it implied that he promised to lobby Sandberg for Li in return.

So, what was Sandberg's attitude? Sandberg had come out to talk for Pao Yue-Kong and let Li Ka-shing give up the Wharf, but if Sandberg could transfer the 90 million shares of Hutchison Whampoa to Li Ka-shing just because of this sentiment, it would be too much to underestimate the Executive Vice Chairman of HSBC.

This lofty banker's position played a decisive role. If he made decisions only according to human relationships, how could HSBC still exist? How could he still hold the position of Executive Vice Chairman?

His purpose was simple. As a bank with the largest number of shares of Hutchison Whampoa, he would not sell the stock to practice arbitrage. He just hoped that the people in charge of Hutchison Whampoa could run it better.

Li Ka-shing was indeed a suitable candidate, not only for bringing a small factory in a far corner of Hong Kong to the Central District, but for also transforming the dilapidated Cheung Kong Plastic Factory into a listed company with both manufacturing and real estate interests. He stood out because of his shrewd business sense, his credible, down-to-earth attitude, and his all-round skills and abilities.

In Sandberg's eyes, Li Ka-shing's defeat of Hongkong Land was due to his business strategies, his shrewdness and scheming, as well as his principle of pursuing win-win business that generated success and profits together with others. It was very clever, but it was also a mysterious approach that many people could not understand.

Just like a product in its initial stages, there was still a long way to go, and it could not demonstrate an immediate price-performance benefit. The next level would be where the value of the product lay.

An ordinary VW Jetta and a luxury Mercedes-Benz could take you to the same place in the same amount of time, but there would be obvious differences in comfort, manoeuvrability, safety and kerb appeal. Likewise, with the Wharf transaction there was an expectation that millions of Hong Kong dollars should 'deliver' in a clear and visible way.

At the same time, skill and finesse in operating an enterprise could often emerge in moments of confrontation. These face-offs revealed the gap between the masters, which would determine their levels of mastery and the ultimate fate of their enterprises.

For example, to cut profits in favor of the other side, we should not only satisfy the other party, but also watch out for our own bottom line. If the other party was not satisfied, the agreement might not be signed. How could you succeed if you lost sight of your bottom line? Without profits, your agreement would lose its fundamental meaning.

Li Ka-shing cut the profits just right, satisfying MTR while also making a lot of money for himself. This required the wisdom of the operators, which was not only needed by Sandberg, but also by the leadership of Hutchison Whampoa.

Of course, Pao Yue-Kong's lobbying was also an essential factor. What great vision the shipping tycoon had! He could appreciate this rookie's foray into big-stakes real estate and would be glad to personally lobby for him. Sandberg knew that Li Ka-shing had been deeply appreciated by Pao Yue-Kong.

At that time, Li was already one of Hong Kong's mega-millionaires, as evidenced by the position of Cheung Kong Holdings in the Central District. But he carried himself with no pomp or formality – he would go out dressed in simple clothes, seldom spoke in public, and let his actions speak for themselves. He was known to be completely trustworthy and would never go back on his word.

There are many stories of how Li Ka-shing conducted himself. In one instance, when he was still making plastic flowers, a former customer came to look for him. This man was an old friend from when Li was a salesman and manager in the previous plastic factory. Recall that when he left to open his own company, he'd promised his former boss, "In the future, my products may overlap with yours, but I will never develop my business with your customers."

Although the new Cheung Kong Plastic Factory desperately needed business, Li Ka-shing kept his promise and respectfully declined to work with the old customers.

This was precious in the Hong Kong business community, where self-interest always ranked first. Above all, Li Ka-shing was known for his personal integrity.

Yet, Li never lacked courage and resolution. Since he said he would duke it out with Hongkong Land, he dared to compete for construction rights for the over-track buildings. He decided to take the Wharf, but he transferred it to Pao Yue-Kong at a very critical moment. Every story about him was colorful and astounding.

Therefore, Li Ka-shing was actually the best person in the eyes of Sandberg. At such a perfect and timely moment, who could take over Hutchison Whampoa except Li Ka-shing?

On the evening of 23 September 1979, the meeting room of Cheung Kong Holdings' headquarters, on the 21st floor of the China Building, was brilliantly illuminated and all seats there were occupied. The cameras in the hands of the reporters flashed frequently. Li Ka-shing walked to the rostrum, looked around the hushed press gallery and cleared his throat. "Without affecting the original business of Cheung Kong Holdings, our company has made a great breakthrough," he said. "Cheung Kong Holdings purchased 90 million ordinary shares of Hutchison Whampoa Limited held by HSBC at the price of HK$7.1 per share."

Although this news had already been disclosed, Li Ka-shing's pronouncement drew thunderous applause from the assembled journalists.

This was a great event for the business community in Hong Kong. From then on, Li Ka-shing was known as 'Superman Li' at home and abroad.

3. SUPERMAN LI

After the acquisition of Hutchison Whampoa was settled, the former Chairman of the Board, Edmond Wai Leung Ho, said reluctantly, "Li Ka-shing just used $24 million as a deposit to get an asset worth more than $1 billion."

Moreover, they did not confront each other with daggers, but put an end to the battle without shedding a drop of blood.

Li Ka-shing's steady footsteps already echoed in the corridors of Hutchison Whampoa, and on 1 January 1981 he officially became its Chairman of the Board, and the first Chinese leader of the company. The long-independent British company would over time become a subsidiary of the Chinese born and bred Cheung Kong Holdings.

Like the Yangtze River, it would not refuse any stream joining in.

To sum up Li's strategic approach, 'harmony was the most precious,' 'retreat was the most advantageous' and 'cutting profits was to make more profits.' How simple and unpretentious these ideas were. However, they could be regarded as ingenious, and a model for success in the field of commercial acquisitions.

Afterwards, the Hong Kong media were full of praise for the transaction and Li's skillful management of it all.

The *Hong Kong Economic Journal* had this to say: "At such a low price (HK$127.8 million for the time being), Cheung Kong Holdings can control such a huge company and own such huge assets. This transaction is a great victory for Mr Li Ka-shing. The acquisition of the 90 million Hutchison Whampoa shares was the most successful acquisition done by Cheung Kong Holdings after its listing. It was better than the previous plan of acquiring the Wharf (using less money and controlling more assets). Mr Li Ka-shing is not only a strong man in the real estate sector, but also a hot figure in the stock market."

Here's how *The Times* characterized it: "Over the past year, the Chinese consortia represented by the shipping giant Pao Yue-Kong and the real estate giant Li Ka-shing have scored successive points in major mergers and re-organizations of Hong Kong's business sector, which has made British-owned companies in Hong Kong nervous. As is well-known, Hong Kong is a former British colony. However, the vast majority of Hong Kong's population is still Chinese, while the British, who hold the political and economic lifelines of Hong Kong, are ethnic minorities. Since World War II, especially in the 1960s and 1970s, the economic power of Chinese people has grown rapidly."

It continued: "With the strong China as a backbone, these new Chinese businessmen, like a tiger with wings added, have the courage to openly compete with British businessmen in the market in order to gain greater economic benefits from them, which makes Hong Kong's British businessmen particularly uneasy. Even the large shareholders of the world-famous Jardine Matheson Group have a feeling of stepping into a minefield. British businessmen are not only astonished by this changing world, but also admit that Chinese businessmen such as Pao Yue-Kong and Li Ka-shing can be compared with outstanding members of British business circles."

This was done under watchful eyes, especially among the shareholders of Hutchison Whampoa. They were waiting for what the ambitious new leader would do after acquiring the largest number of shares. How could Hutchison Whampoa, a stranded commercial vessel, be redirected on a new course to the future? They were impartial, and critical, but full of expectations.

Having just arrived at Hutchison Whampoa, Li Ka-shing became an Executive Director with his stock rights. As the largest shareholder, he was firmly in control of the enterprise.

In the eyes of other directors, Li Ka-shing did not show a trace of arrogance, let alone a domineering stance. Not only did he refuse the high director's emoluments offered by the board, but he also paid for the company's inspection and official reception himself. He was never bossy towards board members, but instead listened to the opinions of all sides, even those shareholders who were suspicious of him.

Li Ka-shing's gentlemanly style conquered the directors of the board first. They all admired this executive director, who had great power but never made a showy display of it. Therefore, they also listened carefully to Li Ka-shing's opinions and suggestions, especially those for the next steps in Hutchison Whampoa's operations, and for the most part supported his proposals.

The original Hutchison Whampoa had great strength, but its front line was too long. It had merged a lot of companies, encompassing some 360 in its heyday. It had also built many new buildings and plots, such as Whampoa Estate, Cosmopolitan Estates, etc. For a time, it seemed that Hutchison Real Estate was blooming everywhere.

But an excessive appetite will inevitably lead to indigestion. In addition to the stock market catastrophe, the oil crisis and the real estate slump, Hutchison Whampoa, which had been overburdened, finally fell into the mud of financial difficulties. It lost HK$200 million in two consecutive fiscal years, which was the main reason why the owners pledged their shares to HSBC.

Li Ka-shing searched for the causes and put forwards corresponding management measures, which quickly helped turn the business around. In his first year in office, he added HK$101 million to Hutchison Whampoa. Four years later, the company would make HK$1.167 billion in net profit, five times as much as in the year when Li came onboard.

In 1989, Hutchison Whampoa's recurrent profit reached HK$3.03 billion. Non-economic profit reached HK$3.05 billion. Net profit alone was over 10 times more than it had been 10 years earlier.

All the grim faces and critical eyes disappeared from the boardroom, replaced by admiration and modesty. By then Edmond had already ceded the position of Chairman of the Board. And Li Ka-shing did not compete with any directors, let alone any shareholders. His modesty and ingenuity eventually conquered everyone. Facts speak louder than words, and the nickname 'Superman Li' spread like wildfire.

However, Li Ka-shing did not like this title. He did not allow his subordinates to call him that and would criticize those who did. When facing the media, he refused to talk about it.

Finally, in 1981, Li Ka-shing talked about this issue head-on and expressed his views.

"Before the age of 20, 100% of the achievements in my career depended on my hard work," he said. "Between the ages of 20 and 30, there were some small foundations in my career. In those 10 years, 10% of the success depended on good luck, and the other 90% still came from hard work. After that, the proportion of opportunities has gradually increased, and now, luck has accounted for almost 30% to 40%."

Li Ka-shing had always been modest. He did not admit that he was a superman but attributed his success to his diligence and good luck.

What did other people think?

Hung Shek said, "Mr Li believed that his early diligence was the stage of capital saving, which is also the concept of 'the first barrel of gold' in the West."

However, there are probably thousands of people who work more than 10 hours a day, 7 days a week, in Hong Kong. Why haven't they been hugely successful after decades of hard work?

From this we can see that Li's belief that diligence is the basis of success is still a reflection of his humility. His good fortune is only an illusion. Li has a knack for identifying opportunities and the ability to persevere. His skill for discovering opportunities has been regarded as 'lucky' by normal people. Many people live a mediocre life because they are not able to distinguish opportunities, have no courage to seize opportunities, or lack the 'first barrel of gold' when facing opportunities. There are also some people who just let the opportunities slip away because they are unwilling to make even the smallest sacrifice.

To 'distinguish' here may be a kind of ability, and then you need to be able to persevere. That's the root of success. To put it simply, to be able to discover opportunities and grasp them firmly is the secret of success.

4. RIGHT-HAND MEN

Actually, Li Ka-shing was not a superman but a normal person. However, among ordinary people, he was smarter, more hardworking, more generous, more far-sighted, more pragmatic and more sociable.

When Cheung Kong Factory was being built, he was both a father and a mother to the effort. He could manage both technology and sales work at the same time.

He just undertook the whole thing. But then Cheung Kong Industries became Cheung Kong Holdings. After acquiring Hutchison Whampoa Limited, it suddenly had thousands of employees and countless projects. Its business scope expanded from plastic and real estate to logistics, warehousing, docks, public transportation, hotels and more.

Even if Li Ka-shing had three heads and six arms, he would not have been able to manage the huge commercial empire alone. Undoubtedly, he had to build a team. So how should he build this team?

Here's what Li himself had to say on the matter: "Cheung Kong Holdings was so named because we wanted it to be like the Yangtze River, which never refuses any small streams. Only when you are generous and open-minded can you accept all streams. If there were no small streams, how could the Yangtze River come into being? Only with such a broad mind can people restrain themselves from thinking that they are outstanding enough. Recognizing the strengths of others and getting help from others are in accordance with the ancient saying that tolerance is great. If there weren't so many people working for me today, I couldn't cope with so many things, even if I had three heads and six arms. So the key to success is to have someone help you and be willing to work with you. That's my philosophy."

His language was simple but profound. This was the essence of Li Ka-shing – plain but shrewd. There were people who 'helped' him and were 'willing' to do that. That was his skill in managing his subordinates. That was the secret of his team.

There were three key points.

First, he attached great importance to friendship, and treated others leniently.

He had two right-hand men who had followed him for many years. One was Shing Chung-sing, and the other was Chow Chin-wo. The former managed production for him and the latter dealt with finance. They had been conscientious and loyal for over a decade. Li Ka-shing placed them in successive vice-president positions on the board of directors, with presumably huge salaries. Later, when Shing Chung-sing's family immigrated to Canada, Li Ka-shing offered them great assistance and hosted a banquet to see his production chief off.

All of Li's actions had a strong human touch. Seeing this, many people were deeply impressed by their boss and would praise his kindness.

Cheung Kong Factory mainly produced plastic flowers. Later, plastic flowers went out of style and the profits became very thin. But Cheung Kong Factory still stayed in operation. Some reporters felt this was strange. After all, Cheung Kong Holdings could make a lot of money through its many other projects. Why not shut down the operation?

"An enterprise is like a family," Li explained. "The employees have all contributed a lot to the company, so they deserve such treatment. Now they are getting on in years. As the younger generation, we should take the responsibility to look after them."

Someone said, "Mr Li's spirit is precious. Many bosses will kick away their employees when they get old, but you are different. These employees used to depend on you to support themselves. Now that the factory is gone, you still help them."

Li Ka-shing replied, "You should not talk like that. It is the old-fashioned boss's opinion that employees are supported by bosses. Actually, it is the employees that support the boss and company."

This was what Li Ka-shing was like. So few members of his team left. There were a lot of people who followed him from the beginning to the end.

Second, Li kept pace with the times and chose all types of talents.

From a small factory in Shau Kei Wan to Cheung Kong Holdings in the Central District, and then to the acquisition of Hutchison Whampoa, his company became a large listed enterprise that had grown numerous times in scale. Obviously, many people could not keep up with the situation, especially after the listing. Many new ideas and new ways were available in the new management talents Li Ka-shing would hire.

First, there was Canning Fok, who graduated from the University of Hong Kong and then went to the United States for further study. In 1979, he returned to Hong Kong for part-time study and passed the exam for the Association of Chartered Certified Accountants in the Commonwealth of Australia. Li Ka-shing took note of him and made him the company's Director of Accounting. Later, he was named Director of Cheung Kong Holdings, and was promoted to Deputy Managing Director two years later, at just 35 years of age.

So apparent was Canning's financial acumen that one Hong Kong newspaper called him "a man full of money-making cells." Canning planned or participated in the decision-making on all kinds of businesses, such as major investments, stock issuance, bank loans, bond exchange and Cheung Kong Holdings' other financial dealings.

Each of these projects represented billions of dollars in capital, and losses and gains would depend on the vision and courage of the decision-makers. Canning's significant position in Cheung Kong Holdings, and in Li Ka-shing's heart, could be seen from this.

Another young man worth mentioning was Chau Nin-mao, who was Chow Chin-wo's son. Li Ka-shing sent him to England to study law, and when he graduated and returned to Hong Kong, Li appointed him spokesman for the company. He achieved excellent results in 1983 and was elected to a director's position. In 1985, he was promoted to Deputy Managing Director, when he was only in his early 30s.

As Deputy Managing Director, Chau Nin-mao was mainly responsible for the real estate development of Cheung Kong Holdings. At that time, he planned and implemented the development of many large residential districts, such as Laguna City in Cha Kwo Ling, Sceneway Garden in Lam Tin, South Horizons in Ap Lei Chau and Lake Ka Garden in Tin Shui Wai. He did a commendable job and was heaped with praise.

Hong Kong's official land had an auction system. In every auction season, Chau Nin-mao would attend the auction for Li Ka-shing. He would dress well and seem like a gentle scholar. However, in the face of decision-making and challenges, he would show a general's demeanor. He would be resolute in deciding whether to make a purchase or give it up. The media commented that he'd clearly been taught by 'Superman Li,' who could advance or retreat flawlessly and make money without doing evil.

While someone managed finance for Li Ka-shing, and someone else managed his real estate, another general on his team is worth mentioning. Hung Siu-Lin – Katherine – began working for Li in the late 1960s, as his secretary. Later, she became a director of Cheung Kong Holdings.

Katherine was well mannered, enthusiastic and eloquent. She was mainly responsible for the sales of Cheung Kong Holdings' buildings and the listings of the sale situations. She would do all kinds of work by herself, no matter how trivial it was.

The headquarters of Cheung Kong Holdings was the centre of a vast business empire, with thousands of employees and a peak asset value of more than HK$200 billion. All kinds of matters would be channeled through Katherine. A thorough pragmatist, she would take care of things personally, down to conducting a messenger's interview, ordering drinks for a meeting or booking the hotel where a client would stay, making sure that everything was well prepared.

These three people constituted Li Ka-shing's 'three-in-hand' at Cheung Kong Holdings, who took on different tasks and worked together towards the same direction. Of course, behind these three, there were still many other managers, who constituted a huge and effective management layer of Cheung Kong Holdings. In addition, there were three other people, who constituted the think tank and were called 'guest managers' by Li Ka-shing. They did not belong to Cheung Kong Holdings, but were inextricably linked with it: Charles Lee Yeh-kwong, Philip L. Tose and Simon Murray.

Charles Lee Yeh-kwong, a senior lawyer and a licensed Commonwealth accountant, was a talented professional with a high reputation in Hong Kong. In the later expansion of Cheung Kong Holdings, Charles Lee made a lot of efforts. His professional knowledge of finance and laws helped solve many practical problems for Li Ka-shing.

Then there was Philip L. Tose, a British known as the 'securities expert.' He originally worked in London Securities Brokerage and then went to DBS Vickers as the representative of Hong Kong. During this period, he and Li Ka-shing formed an indissoluble bond. Philip L. Tose was famous as Li Ka-shing's stockbroker, who guided and participated in the many stock market acquisition battles of Cheung Kong Holdings, and managed the stock trading of Cheung Kong Holdings and Li Ka-shing.

These people gathered together to serve Cheung Kong Holdings, which reflected Li Ka-shing's personal charisma from the side. It also showed that Li Ka-shing treated people well and managed his subordinates skillfully. *Next Magazine* analyzed this in the article, 'Li Ka-shing's Right-Hand Man':

> In contrast, some of the richest people in their careers are not as prosperous as Li Ka-shing. If we have to say that they have any shortcomings, it is that they often do not know how to appoint talents, which hinders the development of their enterprises. If we look around the listed companies in Hong Kong, although many companies have a lot of assets, they still cannot free themselves from the family management.

After Li Ka-shing's careful construction, the management mode of modern enterprises was completely adopted in Cheung Kong Holdings. Simon Murray once said, "The industrial management of Cheung Kong Holdings combines the advantages of the old, the middle-aged and the young, and has both Chinese and Western colors. It is an effective management model."

And who was Simon Murray? He was an Englishman, who was regarded by Ren Zhengfei, the boss of Huawei, a later Chinese enterprise, as his teacher. He was closely related to Li Ka-shing and played an important role in the development of Cheung Kong Holdings.

CHAPTER

ACQUISITION OF THE HONGKONG ELECTRIC COMPANY, LIMITED

1. SIMON MURRAY

Simon Murray was both a soldier and a businessman, who combined the characteristics of an adventurer and a financier. He was a pioneering and enterprising modern entrepreneur whose vision was at once forwards-looking and comprehensive.

As mentioned above, Li Ka-shing's management team in Cheung Kong Holdings not only combined old, middle-aged and young employees within a rational structure, but also integrated both Chinese and Western features, enabling it to be affected by both Confucian traditions and Western cultures. Murray was one of the representatives – perhaps the most important representative – of the Western side.

First, let's look at his experience.

Born in Leicester, in the English Midlands, on 25 March 1940, Murray was a soldier, businessman and explorer. When he was young, he served in the French Foreign Legion and was stationed in Algeria. After retiring from the military, he went to the Far East to do business and joined Hong Kong's Jardine Matheson. He sold air conditioners and elevators before leaving to set up his own company. Later, he became CEO of Hutchison Whampoa, got along well with Li Ka-shing and controlled a series of large-scale operations.

He was arguably Li Ka-shing's most important assistant. Li once described their relationship: "Listen, Simon, we won't do anything you don't want to do. And we won't do anything I don't want to do, either. Only when we both want to do it, we do it. I am the one who drives the car. And he will sit in the back seat and tell me where to go."

In 1984, Li Ka-shing acquired Murray's company and asked him to become Director and General Manager of Hutchison Whampoa. This was a clear reflection of how Li appreciated and relied on him.

Beyond his business achievements, Murray always sought out adventure. At the age of 60, he walked 254 kilometres through the Sahara Desert. At 63, he hiked more than a thousand kilometres from Greater Bay, Antarctica, to the Antarctic Pole without supplies. When Murray was 72, Huawei's Ren Zhengfei visited him in London. Sitting in his office, Murray pointed to the 1,680-foot FRP building opposite him and said, "Three days ago, I climbed down by a rope from there."

In the late 1970s, when Li Ka-shing was president of Cheung Kong Holdings, Murray was still an air conditioner salesman for Jardine Matheson. One day the Englishman came to the headquarters of Cheung Kong Holdings and declared that he had to see Li Ka-shing. He was not very tall, and wore a vest and a checked shirt, but would impress others with his sharp eyes. His piercing stare would make people uncomfortable after a few seconds, but as soon as he opened his mouth, his affinity would bring them closer to him.

"Chairman Li, I heard that you were born in the year of the dragon, weren't you?" Murray said as he shook Li Ka-shing's hand. A smile rose on his face, and at that moment, his eyes seemed to overflow with laughter.

An inexplicable feeling of goodwill rose in Li Ka-shing's heart. He also broke into a smile, waved his hand, and told his visitor, "Please have a seat. Tea or coffee?"

"Thank you, Chairman Li," he replied. "We are both descendants of the dragon. So, tea, please!"

It was true that Murray had also been born in the year of the dragon. He was 12 years younger than Li Ka-shing. In a show of deferential respect, he cupped one hand in the other and said, "Elder Brother!"

Li Ka-shing was surprised that this Westerner understood traditional Chinese etiquette. Moreover, he even knew that Li Ka-shing was born in the year of the dragon. It seemed that he had done his homework, and it seemed that Li Ka-shing had found himself in this Englishman. So, he talked with Murray with great interest.

From that time on, Li Ka-shing and Simon Murray became friends. Li was impressed that this man was not only familiar with business and sales, but seemed to possess wide-ranging knowledge. Moreover, his stubbornness and brave spirit were the most valuable qualities for entrepreneurs who fought the daily fight in business circles. Later, in 1984, after Murray and others had set up a company together, Li Ka-shing's office called him in for a meeting. Li bought his company and appointed him Director and General Manager of Hutchison Whampoa.

Murray believed that only leaders who let people follow voluntarily were real leaders. "Leaders also need to be knowledgeable, visionary, courageous and have a clear understanding of where they are heading," he said. Specifically, he was talking about Li Ka-shing.

Murray's Chinese name, Ma Shimin, refers to 'people for the world.' After arriving in Hong Kong, he carefully studied all of the transaction processes and gradually became familiar with the business environment. Moreover, he was extremely smart, and quickly mastered the game of commerce.

He also had an unconventional backstory, which might help us to better understand this legend.

In 1990, China's carrier rocket CZ-3 sent the AsiaSat 1 satellite into orbit. This was the first time that China had conducted an international commercial launch, and it propelled China's space program into the world market. But few people knew that Murray was one of the hands behind this event.

This satellite had an unusual history. Its predecessor was a communications satellite in geostationary orbit, designed by Hughes Aircraft of the United States. In February 1984, the NASA space shuttle Challenger was launched, carrying the satellite into orbit. After being deployed by the shuttle, the satellite's engine failed to ignite and push it into the proper position, rendering the project a failure. The insurer, Lloyd's, paid $75 million in premiums and acquired ownership of the wayward satellite.

Fortunately, the ground tracking station that monitored the satellite's location found it to be in good condition. After weighing the cost, risks and potential benefits, Lloyd's paid Hughes and NASA $2.75 million to recovery the satellite. In November 1984, the Space Shuttle Discovery flew to within nine metres of the drifting satellite. Two astronauts spacewalked out of the cabin and spent more than six hours guiding the satellite into the cargo hold.

Back on Earth, the satellite was sent to Hughes, where experts thoroughly inspected it. Proposals for renovation, overhaul and re-launch were submitted to Lloyd's in April 1985.

Lloyd's sold the satellite to a telecoms company for $50 million, but the business went bankrupt and the satellite was returned to the insurer. Later, Asia Satellite Telecommunications Holdings, Limited – also called AsiaSat

– purchased the satellite, renamed it AsiaSat 1, and modified it to provide service in the Asian market. Finally, the re-launch into orbit was completed by the China Great Wall Company's CZ-3 rocket.

At that time, Simon Murray was Managing Director of Hutchison Whampoa and Co-Chairman of AsiaSat. He wanted to persuade the US government to agree to let China's low-cost rockets participate in bidding for launching, which would help the US sell more satellites. He had to persuade the Coordinating Committee for Multilateral Export Controls – the international organization through which the US and its allies coordinate and monitor the sale of strategic technology to communist countries – to allow China to launch the satellite. He also had to convince the Chinese government to let the US Marine Corps physically escort the satellite to China.

It was a pioneering event, especially in 1989 and 1990. The miracle eventually happened. CITIC Group, China's state-owned investment company, did a lot of work associated with the deal. Murray, as Co-Chairman of AsiaSat, had ultimate responsibility for pulling it all off, which showcased his abilities.

In his preface to Murray's autobiography, Ren Zhengfei wrote: "Simon Murray is a very good example for the contemporary youth in today's fast-growing China. For me, he's a real teacher. I don't know how many businesses he's got in the world or how he allocates his time. There are still a lot of things for me to learn."

Murray's book was titled *Legionnaire: Five Years in the French Foreign Legion*. The subtitle was, *From a Tough General to a Giant Entrepreneur*.

2. ACQUISITION OF THE HONGKONG ELECTRIC COMPANY, LIMITED

Li Ka-shing's acquisition of the Hong Kong Electric Company, Limited, was one of the four major battles in which Chinese investment marched into British-funded companies.

Because of the colonial nature of Hong Kong, British capital had always been the first to control its economic lifeline. The major businesses, that the people of Hong Kong called 'foreign companies,' were all in the hands of the British. In terms of power supply in Hong Kong, the two major power companies were Hongkong Electric Company and CLP Group. The former, as a British holding company, was sponsored by Paul Chater, a prominent British-Indian businessman with extensive interests in Hong Kong. The latter was controlled by the British-Hong Kong billionaire Michael Kadoorie's family.

In the 1970s, the rise of Chinese businessmen challenged the areas controlled by British businessmen. Pao Yue-Kong bought the Wharf and Li Ka-shing bought Hutchison Whampoa. These acquisitions sent shockwaves rippling back to the UK.

Hongkong Electric Company had long supplied electricity to the whole of Hong Kong, so the Hong Kong government attached great importance to it. To encourage electricity use, the company introduced a charging system whereby the more people used, the cheaper it would be. The company was known to generate steady profits; as long as people used electricity, those profits would flow.

When Murray arrived at Hutchison Whampoa, he suggested to Li Ka-shing that more projects should be developed to generate more revenue streams, making Cheung Kong Holdings stronger.

Indeed, in Cheung Kong Holdings' business scope, energy was a blank area. But energy was an indispensable resource for modern industry and people's lives. Just as people must eat, they consume energy to get on with life. To control energy was not only a long-term goal for the enterprise but also a practical interest. It was a very important step. In fact, how had Li Ka-shing not seen this before? The acquisition of Hutchison Whampoa had added many new projects to Cheung Kong Holdings, but real estate remained as its primary area of business. This was a traditional industry, but not a growing one.

Although Li Ka-shing and Murray were optimistic about the future of the Hongkong Electric Company, Li, as a driver, never became impatient or blind. He was observing, studying and waiting for the time when the other party exhibited weaknesses.

So, who was the other party? It turned out to be his old rival, Hongkong Land.

Hongkong Land had also taken a fancy to the Hongkong Electric Company. As an old player in the commercial world, the real estate giant understood how valuable the stable income of Hongkong Electric Company was. In addition, Hongkong Land, with its vast wealth, made such a generous offer for the power company that nobody could compete with it, which surprised the whole business community.

In April 1982, after a long period of preparation, Hongkong Land had amassed enough 'silver bullets' and took action. A cloud of smoke floated over Hong Kong's stock market, and the 'silver bullets' prepared by Hongkong Land fell like raindrops. It first acquired a HK$222 million stake in Hongkong Electric Company at a high price of HK$6.13 per share.

Just as everyone was struck dumb with astonishment, Hongkong Electric Company took this opportunity to push its share price up, while Hongkong Land set its own limit at HK$9.4 and acquired 12 million warrants to purchase shares.

When the smoke had cleared, however, people were surprised to find that Cheung Kong Holdings had not intervened in this battle. People had assumed that many companies wanted a piece of the power company. It was likely that Cheung Kong Holdings, Carrian Holdings and other powerful companies would compete for it, setting up a bitter battle. Instead, the result was shocking. Li Ka-shing did not take any action. Nor did Carrian Holdings, owing to its inferior strength.

The battle to acquire the Hongkong Electric Company was in the end a one-man show, with Hongkong Land taking the prize. The victor was jubilant.

As for the huge debt associated with the purchase, it would be erased by Hong Kong's ever rising land prices as Hongkong Land went on to develop Exchange Square, in the most expensive section of central Hong Kong.

In fact, Hongkong Land had already shouldered HK$16 billion in debt with the acquisition. As a longtime real estate company, could the powerful Jardine family not know the risks?

An article, headlined 'The Change of Situation in the Acquisition of Hongkong Electric Company,' provides some insight:

"Originally, as long as the real estate market is good, and the economic situation is prosperous, large debts will not be a problem. With abundant capital and the King Land of Central Hong Kong in its hands, Hongkong Land will have no worries about making money. Unfortunately, the fall of Mrs Thatcher in Beijing has smashed the confidence of Hong Kong's people into pieces."

The so-called 'change of situation' meant different things to different people. As far as Hongkong Land was concerned, the situation was changed from a positive trend to a negative trend. But for Li Ka-shing's Cheung Kong Holdings, it was a good opportunity that he had been waiting for a long time.

Of course, it would be a little far-fetched to say that Li Ka-shing had foreseen such an outcome when Hongkong Land took possession of the Hongkong Electric Company. After all, anticipating the future was all but impossible, especially when there were no obvious signs of what was to come. Otherwise, the beaten-down Chater family would not have made such a decision so easily.

However, Li Ka-shing would always make careful plans before taking action. He always paid attention to the political situation. He'd appointed Simon Murray the head of Hutchison Whampoa because Murray had stayed in Jardine Matheson, and knew it well. He therefore would know the opponent when heading into battle. Murray told Li that the Jardine companies had a fatal weakness: 'communist phobia.'

The news that Beijing would restore Hong Kong's sovereignty in 1997 generated shockwaves. In particular, Hongkong Land, whose British owner had already been in heavy debt, was now facing the last straw.

The real estate industry collapsed in an instant, and recently completed buildings lost their tenants. The huge loans the developers owed to banks were not only in default, but the daily interest they generated was equal to the value of a whole building.

In 1983, Hongkong Land suffered a loss of HK$1.3 billion. This impacted the whole Jardine system, whose fiscal profits fell by 80% that year. The situation reached an unbearable level, leaving Jardine Matheson in disarray. Jardine's major shareholder since the 1870s, the Keswick family, publicly denounced David Kennedy Newbigging, the Chairman of Hongkong Land, for his mistakes. He had no choice but to resign.

Simon Keswick's family appointed him Chairman of Jardine Matheson and Hongkong Land. Could this nobleman from Britain, who was thrust into this position under extreme circumstances, reverse Hongkong Land's seemingly passive demise? What he took over was not only the chairmanship of Jardine Matheson and Hongkong Land, but heavy bank debts. Unless he had an ability to make gold out of stone, he would have many difficulties diversifying his business, starting afresh and creating new brilliance.

In fact, with Simon Murray's strong encouragement, Li Ka-shing never stopped coveting the Hongkong Electric Company. But why did he not take any action? The reason was that the fire from Hongkong Land was too fierce. He just did not want to pick chestnuts from the fire. When Hongkong Land was in trouble and the Keswicks condemned Newbigging, he could have made a takeover move, but he still did not act.

Murray was puzzled, but Li told him that he did not want Newbigging to be too embarrassed. He had been with Jardine Matheson for 30 years, and in the Chairman's office for eight years. Jardine Matheson had lost the Wharf on Newbigging's watch and now he'd lost the Hongkong Electric Company, which cast a shadow over his reputation.

Li believed that things would be sorted out through negotiations, as he realized that sooner or later Hongkong Land would sell the Hongkong Electric Company. Hongkong Land had no other way to go, even if Simon Keswick had been put in charge.

Of course, Li Ka-shing did his research on Keswick. The young man had joined Jardine Matheson in 1962 and initially worked in its overseas operations. In early 1982, Keswick was transferred to Hong Kong, and that year became the company's Managing Director. He persuaded other directors to make trouble for Newbigging, which put Hongkong Land's Chairman in a tough position. With the collapse of the real estate industry, Newbigging could only choose to take the blame and resign, while Keswick ascended to the Chairman's throne of Jardine Matheson and Hongkong Land.

In order to defeat Hongkong Land again and get the Hongkong Electric Company from them, Li Ka-shing could not help focusing his eyes on the powerful Englishman who had just turned 40.

3. SIMON KESWICK

Keswick was born in Winchester, England, in 1942. When he was a teenager, he attended Eton College and later Trinity College, Cambridge. He went on to travel the world and participate in the family business. He could be regarded as quite experienced. When he moved to

Hong Kong, he became Managing Director of Jardine Matheson, signaling that he was no longer the playboy he had been in the past. After Newbigging resigned, he was appointed President of Hongkong Land, which not only implied his family's trust in him, but also showed his ability.

When Keswick became President, he immediately started to put his house in order, clean up the debt crisis and revitalize Jardine Matheson. He launched a self-help and loan repayment package, the core of which was to sell some of his overseas assets and non-core business in Hong Kong.

In Hong Kong, the core business of Jardine Matheson was real estate. Hongkong Land was Jardine's flagship company, at the centre of it all. At present, however, Hongkong Land was in heavy debt. It became apparent that in shedding non-core assets, the Hongkong Electric Company would be put into play.

In fact, when Newbigging was in power, Li Ka-shing had offered to buy the Hongkong Electric Company. Newbigging rejected his offer. Now, however, there would be no better suitor than Li Ka-shing – no potential buyer was stronger than Cheung Kong Holdings.

In Keswick's mind, Li Ka-shing was sure to get the Hongkong Electric Company, so he signaled his intent to sell and waited for Li to call. However, like the frightening tranquility on the battlefield on the eve of war, everything was surprisingly quiet.

Keswick was upset, as his recovery plan would go bankrupt if he failed to sell the Hongkong Electric Company. How could he save his Hongkong Land if this happened? And if Hongkong Land was not secured, would he be ousted from his chairmanship of the real estate company and Jardine Matheson?

Thinking of this, Keswick became frightened. He grabbed the phone, hesitated for a long time, and finally hung up. Instead, he dispatched an assistant to the headquarters of Cheung Kong Holdings on Queen's Road.

Through its patents and other protections, the Hongkong Electric Company was immune to competition as it provided electricity to Hong Kong's millions. It could be said that this company was able to ensure a steady yield every year, no matter what happened. Had it not been for too much debt owed by Hongkong Land, the Hongkong Electric Company's income would be all but uninterruptable. But with the debt burden hanging over his head, Keswick had little choice but to offer up his precious Hongkong Electric Company.

What was Li Ka-shing's reaction? "Unlike buying antiques," he said at the time, "we do not have the mentality that we must buy it in this situation."

It was this mindset that enabled him to take the tense situation calmly and wait for Keswick's special envoy to come calling. In fact, Li and Murray carefully had analyzed the Hongkong Land situation and had studied the psychology and characteristics of Keswick. Their research led to a strategy of waiting in patience.

It was clear that repayment of Hongkong Land's staggering debt required the sale of the Hongkong Electric Company. The power company was highly valued and would bring a good price. Furthermore, Keswick had squeezed out Newbigging and became the head of Jardine Matheson. He had a desire to succeed. His top priority was to resolve Hongkong Land's debt crisis and set Jardine Matheson on the road to recovery.

In addition to these factors, in Hong Kong at that time, Cheung Kong Holdings had the strength and courage to buy the Hongkong Electric Company.

Cheung Kong Holdings had opened its door to the deal. Li Ka-shing sat waiting with Murray, his strategic advisor, at his side. Sure enough, at the moment they expected, the footsteps of Keswick's assistant sounded. The front desk informed them that a representative of Jardine Matheson had come to visit Chairman Li.

"Please," Li said, smiling at Murray, "show him in."

This is how the *Hong Kong Economic Journal Monthly* described the events that unfolded:

"At 7 pm on Monday, January 21, 1985, many offices in the Central District were empty. Crowds and cars on the street had long been dispersed, but the leader of Hongkong Land was still troubled by the high debt, so he had to send his staff to the office of Li Ka-shing, Chairman of Hutchison Whampoa Co., Ltd., and Cheung Kong Holdings, to discuss the transfer of shares in Hongkong Electric Company. About 16 hours later, Hutchison Whampoa decided to invest HK$2.9 billion to acquire the 34.6% of Hongkong Electric Company's ownership possessed by Hongkong Land. This was the first large-scale acquisition on the Hong Kong stock market after the Sino-British talks."

Later, Murray described Li as follows: "Li Ka-shing combines the advantages of Chinese and European businessmen. Like European and American businessmen, Li Ka-shing can comprehensively analyze the acquisition targets, and then shake hands with them to implement the transaction. This is an Oriental business mode, which is simple and straightforward."

Hammering out the deal took 16 hours, eight of which were spent researching proposals.

This demonstrated that Li Ka-shing had the caution of Western businessmen and the boldness of Eastern people. He showed himself to be smart and capable, simple and generous.

Keswick received a call, advising him that the Hongkong Electric Company transaction had been concluded. Following a long and restless night, he threw down the phone and took a deep breath, clapping his hands. He had survived the race and was still qualified to sit at the top of Jardine Matheson.

Li Ka-shing's actions matched his words. The agreement called for payment of HK$2.9 billion by 23 February. However, Li delivered Keswick a cheque for the full amount nearly a month early – on 1 February – which moved Keswick. After all, this was a rough-and-tumble commercial world, and the daily interest on HK$2.9 billion would have been a huge amount.

Keswick was also a fastidious man of principles. He immediately sent the HK$12 million in interest that would have accrued to Cheung Kong Holdings. Li Ka-shing nodded and quietly praised the English gentleman's great demeanor. In an equal show of integrity, he took only HK$4 million and returned the remaining HK$8 million to Hongkong Land.

Throughout this battle, Li Ka-shing displayed strategic brilliance and strength of will, as well as generosity and respect.

As noted by the *Hong Kong Economic Journal Monthly*, it was the first large-scale acquisition after the Sino-British talks. This showed people how determined Li Ka-shing was and how his predictions about Hong Kong's future had come to pass. Because of the influence of Li Ka-shing and Cheung Kong Holdings in Hong Kong, this acquisition played a key role in stabilizing Hong Kong's public mood and overall economy.

Hongkong Land purchased the Hongkong Electric Company at a 31% premium over the going market rate. Li Ka-shing purchased it at HK$6.4 (following a market price that was HK$7.4 the day before) in the name of Hutchison Whampoa. From that day forwards, Hutchison Whampoa was the controlling shareholder. Li immediately appointed Murray Chairman of the power company, ceding him overall operational control.

Its business range was also expanded from real estate to telecommunications, container terminals, retail, power supply and energy.

In January 1986, the market value of Hutchison Whampoa – which had been HK$6.2 billion in 1979 – grew to HK$14.15 billion. Over the same period, the market value of its parent company, Cheung Kong Holdings, was HK$7.7 billion. The market value of Hutchison Whampoa was nearly twice that of its parent company, making it the flagship of Cheung Kong Holdings' vast portfolio.

In 1979, Li Ka-shing bought 22% of Hutchison Whampoa's equity from HSBC for HK$7.1 per share, paying more than HK$600 million in total. In 1989, it made a net profit of HK$3.05 billion, giving the company a valuation of HK$6.08 billion, 10 times more than its cost.

During this period, under Murray's oversight, the Hongkong Electric Company moved its non-electric business to a new listed company named Cavendish International Holdings. Then Murray bought 23.5% of the shares from Hutchison Whampoa and the new holding company became the parent company of the Hongkong Electric Company. Murray served as Chairman of Cavendish International Holdings.

It was under Murray's leadership that Hutchison Whampoa of Cheung Kong Holdings' system could achieve such remarkable things. Li Ka-shing's strategy and Murray's management complemented each other and pushed the fortunes of Cheung Kong Holdings ever higher.

4. AUCTION MART

Land in Hong Kong needed to be auctioned, with professional auctioneers handling the proceedings. It was also like a battlefield, with the circulation of tens of millions of dollars and success or failure being decided in a flash.

The generals seemed calm in the midst of such dealings, but in fact there were rolling waves in their hearts, for millions could be lost. High stakes purchase decisions had to be made at a moment's notice, or there would be someone else ready to bid.

Ancient people once said that one needed to be calm when confronting every major event. They viewed calmness as a kind of cultivation, temperament, realm and wisdom. In the face of major events, only a calm mind could think soberly, judge correctly, act peacefully and face all kinds of challenges unperturbed. Especially in the impetuous auction mart, calmness was the key to winning.

Some people would shout like gamblers in the auction mart, especially as the price was rising and gradually reaching a climax. Some bidders, because of their strong self-esteem, would put their interests behind them for a time, trying to overwhelm their opponents with higher bids. As a result, they could only gain temporary satisfaction, and what they bought was a hot potato.

Li Ka-shing once said, "In the land auction marts, we must not show the attitude of bidding for antiques. We must learn to go step-by-step."

This is because the two kinds of bidding were essentially different. Li explained it this way: "Most of the time, there are very few antiques. There could be only one of something in the whole world. So, when bidding for antiques, it is primarily based on their own financial strength. But when bidding for land, we do not have to stick to one enterprise or one plot because bidders have a wide range of options. Even if they do not get this piece of land, they can also bid for another piece. In short, the ultimate goal is to use the land to make profits."

This was a real businessman. He would never forget that making profit was the first goal. It was so childish to care about one's face or self-esteem. It would be difficult for such a self-absorbed person to become an outstanding talent.

On 27 November 1987, the government auctioned a plot measuring about 219,000 square metres near Kowloon Bay. Li Ka-shing sat in the auction room with his assistant. His attendance made everyone glance in his direction. Li Ka-shing was expressionless; his eyes were indifferent behind his glasses. No one knew what he would do today. The auction started with a floor price of HK$200 million and a minimum of HK$5 million per bid. That meant that if you wanted to bid, you had to pay at least HK$500 higher than the original price before you were qualified.

The auctioneer hammered and the auction began. Li Ka-shing raised the price a step higher, and then someone shouted a new price again, rapidly taking things to HK$210 million.

The auctioneer's voice was bright, hovering in the hall, "210 million for the first time ..."

Almost all of those attending the auction were Hong Kong real estate tycoons. Several whispered with each other, secretly analyzing the manoeuvring.

The auctioneer's voice came again, "210 million for the second time ..."

Suddenly, a voice flew out from a corner: "215 million!"

When people looked back, it turned out to be Gordon Wu, Chairman of Hopewell Holdings. This really caused a few gasps. Why? As a graduate from the Civil Engineering School of Princeton University, Wu had professional credentials and could be regarded as the pride of the local construction industry. He had set up Hopewell Holdings in Hong Kong and racked up achievements in the local market. He could take a fancy to such a piece of land because he had a clear idea of what to develop there – what kind of houses to build, and how much profit he stood to make. Everyone believed that he must have a well-thought-out-plan, which greatly stimulated the participants in the auction.

Li Ka-shing glanced back at Gordon Wu and smiled slightly. The expression in his eyes seemed to telegraph his thoughts directly to Wu, who immediately smiled back at him to show his understanding. The two had co-operated with each other many times, and Wu had used his professional knowledge to help Li in the past.

But turning around, Li Ka-shing put up his hand and shook the house with his thrilling voice: "300 million!"

In a single move, he pushed the auction price up by eight steps. Everyone looked at each other, and a roar of voices broke out. Though the auctioneer shouted several times for the audience to quieten down, the excited noise grew louder and louder. Through the din, Wu was heard shouting, "335 million!"

It was immediately silent, as Wu lifted the price by 11 steps in one breath.

After a short pause, the auctioneer's voice came again: "335 million for the first time ..."

Only then did everyone regain their wits. Li Ka-shing and Gordon Wu, the two real estate madmen, were saying loud and clear that this plot of land could make a lot of money in the future. Additional bidders followed up and the price continued to climb upwards.

Li Ka-shing's assistant, Chau Nin-mao, and Gordon Wu's assistant, Ho Bing-cheong, sat together. They talked and laughed as the tycoons pushed the bidding to HK$400 million.

The auctioneer took out his handkerchief and wiped the sweat on his forehead. His eyes swept across the hall and finally fell on Li Ka-shing. He seemed to be communicating, "Mr Li, if you don't bid further, it will be settled."

Everyone's eyes fell on Li Ka-shing. He pushed up his glasses, lifted his hand, and in a clear voice said, "495 million!"

Li had just bid more than twice the original price. All eyes turned back to the auctioneer, who knew that nobody could top the offer. So, raising the hammer, he shouted, "495 million, for the first time ... the second time ... the third time!"

When the hammer hit the table, it made a ringing sound that was drowned out by the buzz in the hall. Before the congratulations could begin, Li Ka-shing stood up and said, "This land is won by my cooperation with Mr Gordon Wu. We have decided to make rational and effective use of this land and plan to build a global commercial exhibition hall on it."

Everyone sat down in surprise. It didn't matter so much what the new owner intended to build on the land; the audience was astonished by the cooperation between Li and Wu. They could not help but put their thumbs up in admiration – the two of them were so wise!

At that time, there was much news coverage of Ka-shing's performance in the auction hall. Some called him "the finger that held up the sky," raving that Li could balance the sky on a single outstretched finger. Excitement aside, Li's ability to keep calm in the centre of monumental events, and to succeed as he had, was what most impressed people.

Li Ka-shing developing his small Cheung Kong Factory into today's Cheung Kong Holdings was like a stream flowing out of the glacier and becoming the vast Yangtze River. How could all the hardship, hard work and bravery it took be captured in words? All one can say is that it couldn't have been easy.

Successful people must possess something unusual, besides the fact that they work hard. Li Ka-shing's success could not just be attributable to opportunity. Li in the auction mart, seemingly calm and relaxed, could shock the whole hall with a shout. But behind that shout, how many sleepless nights of research and analysis, how much time to collect information, and how many years of accumulated experience had he leveraged? From this single incident, we can see that he was bringing extraordinary skill and expertise to play.

CHAPTER

TRIUMPHS IN THE STOCK MARKET

1. CHEUNG KONG HOLDINGS GOES PUBLIC

The stock market is a mechanism for buying and selling ownership shares. In 1602, the Dutch traded shares in the British East India Company on Amstel Bridge, which marked the rudimentary beginning of the world's organized stock trading. The formal, modern-day stock market first appeared in the United States. People bought and sold stocks in a fixed place, commonly known as the stock exchange.

As the trade and financial centre in the Far East, Hong Kong originally had four stock exchanges. In 1986, the four were merged into one, namely, Hong Kong Exchanges and Clearing Limited. Although Hong Kong was only a corner of the world, because of its special status, its stock market had a large capacity, with many companies listed.

Becoming 'listed' is the goal of many ambitious business enterprises. To be formally listed on a stock exchange means that ownership of a company's stock – literally, shares of ownership in the company – are openly offered for the public to buy and sell. Listing generates capital, as investors pump money into stock acquisitions, and capital is like blood for enterprises. Without the circulation of this blood, enterprises would die. Listed companies have access to direct funds from the stock market. What they sell here is the future of their enterprises.

If enterprises are esteemed by the public, their future potential can be enormous, and there's a high probability that their stock will grow in value. If the value of stocks doubles, enterprises get a lot of capital, helping guarantee a bright future. This is a beneficent cycle, in which investors 'buy the future.'

Of course, there are companies, and their stocks, that do not perform well. It can be catastrophic for enterprises if their future is not clear, or when their potential fades and stocks fall. This can lead to the complete collapse of underperforming companies.

As the name implies, those who hold shares of stock are a company's 'shareholders.' If the percentage of shares owned by a given shareholder reaches a certain level, he or she could be given a seat on a company's board of directors, or even become Chairman of the Board. Since listed companies operate in a joint stock system, shareholders receive a percentage of the dividends and operating profits of the company. As owners of the company, shareholders profit personally when the company does well.

In addition to the performance of the stock market itself, politics and many other factors can have an impact on the rise and fall of shares. It is difficult to predict the vicissitudes of the stock market. There are periods when the stock market is on the rise, but a sudden drop can spark a market disaster. Therefore, there is a saying that the stock market is a paradise for adventurers and speculators. That certainly speaks to the risks associated with buying and selling stocks.

In fact, every leaf is different. The benevolent see benevolence and the wise see wisdom. As for adventure, some people challenge limits and push themselves to the brink as a personal breakthrough. It was because mankind produced so many seekers and adventurers that so many new lands, and fields of knowledge, could be discovered and explored.

Of course, taking risks is not always reckless, unless one is unprepared. For example, Simon Murray, in order to go hiking in the polar region, had to do considerable planning in advance. This was based on a detailed investigation of the environment, allowing him to prepare the necessary equipment and prepare for emergencies. Even a tiny Swiss army knife could be a lifesaver.

Therefore, only a well-prepared adventure could be called an adventure. The same can be said for being well prepared for a life challenge.

On 1 November 1972, Cheung Kong Holdings was listed on the main board of Hong Kong Exchanges and Clearing Limited. The capital stock requirement was HK$200 million, at HK$2 per share, with a premium of HK$1, totaling HK$3. On that day, 42 million shares in the company were issued on the open market.

Cheung Kong Holdings' move had been carefully planned beforehand. It chose the period when Hong Kong's stock market was on the rise. As an 'up' market is referred to as a bull market, this timing could be called 'a bull-riding listing.' Li Ka-shing had found two underwriters in advance: Schroders and Wardley. At that time, there were still four exchanges. So, the two underwriters sold the shares to investors at the same time.

Due to the long-term reputation and performance of Cheung Kong Holdings, which was well-known to Hong Kong citizens, and with the media's encouragement, there were more than 65 times the requests for shares than there were shares available for sale within 24 hours of the company being listed.

Owing to the popularity of the shares, the underwriters were busy but happy. In order to issue smoothly, they had to adopt the method of drawing lots to deal with the people who rushed to buy. On the first day of listing, the price of Cheung Kong Holdings' shares rose 100%, closing at HK$6. The company's market value effectively doubled on that day, delighting its employees and managers.

Li Ka-shing's wife, Chong Yuet Ming, was appointed Executive Director of the newly listed Cheung Kong Holdings.

Hong Kong's stock market was on the rise, with the value of some stocks climbing even higher than Cheung Kong Holdings' gains. With that came the understanding that Cheung Kong Holdings had appreciated so quickly that a downturn could be just as instantaneous.

Since the listing of Cheung Kong Holdings, Li Ka-shing's mood had not been relaxed. Any rough and tumble turn in the market, and his company's fortunes, would be a big personal blow to him. Stabilizing Cheung Kong Holdings' stocks and giving returns to its shareholders became one of Li's driving objectives.

In 1973, at the recommendation of financial services firm Sun Hung Kai & Co., Limited, Cheung Kong Holdings formally listed in London, with the British Securities Company as its financial adviser and underwriter. And so, it commenced raising funds overseas. This inflow of cash greatly strengthened Cheung Kong Holdings. With funds as its lifeblood, a company could resist risks and expand development.

Next, in June of 1974, Cheung Kong Holdings listed in Canada.

For the Hong Kong business community, this was major news, and something of a shock to the industry. Hong Kong used to be a British colony, so listing in London would not be difficult. However, with its listing in Canada, it was clear that Cheung Kong Holdings' influence extended to North America, and that Li Ka-shing's empire was now well-established overseas.

Li relied mainly on Chow Chin-wo to manage his financial affairs, but he researched and managed many stock transactions himself.

It could be said that there were two main battlefields for Cheung Kong Holdings at that time. One was real estate and the other was the stock market. On these two fronts, Li Ka-shing personally took command, strategized and gained a decisive victory. He had won big in the real estate sector, while being amazingly active in the stock market as well. He had a huge workload every day.

In addition to relying on his team to collect information, he would study the performance of listed companies – how they operated, their management team, even the personality of the head of their board of directors. Moreover, he had to study the political situation at home and abroad. He believed that no economic activity could be separated from the influence of politics, especially government policy that would directly affect the stock market.

Through it all, Li was sensitive and calm. He had his own unique views on the political turmoil Hong Kong had experienced. He would never sail with the wind, nor would he be stubborn. He always used his calmness and intelligence to find different answers from others.

Hong Kong was a tiny piece of land, but it was also a base for mainland China's global imports and exports. It had been a colony of Britain, suspended in the south of China, but it was also a window for China to the outside world. It was fragile but solid. Because of its special position, and for many other reasons, it had become the financial centre of the Far East.

For the business empire Li Ka-shing had built, Hong Kong provided special opportunities for development, and he wasted none of them.

China has its own traditional culture, which an old Taoist saying has captured perfectly: "Quiet as a virgin, active like a rabbit." This means that a person needs to be calm and decisive. He needs to observe quietly and wait steadily for the opportunity. Once an opportunity arises, he should move quickly and take the coveted objective.

To be quiet reflects wisdom, and to be active demonstrates courage. Between the quietness and action, there is a great test for the participants. Especially in the ever-changing stock market, people have the opportunity to act decisively and fight for what they want, but there is always the possibility of both success and failure.

In the stock market, Li Ka-shing controlled the ship of Cheung Kong Holdings, and kept it sailing steadily, but he also took advantage of the opportunities, beating opponents and buying other companies to strengthen the mother ship.

There was no explanation for Li's success other than his extraordinary talent and capability. He was not a 'Superman,' but he was definitely a strong and capable person. His vast wealth was by no means made by sheer luck. He earned it by his perseverance and bold commitment to accumulating experience, knowledge and wisdom.

2. PRIVATIZATION

Once a company is listed, it becomes a legitimate, publicly owned corporation. Because the shares it issues are purchased by the public, the public naturally become its shareholders – its owners – and the listed company becomes a public corporation.

The term 'privatization' refers to large shareholders purchasing all existing shares in a company from small shareholders, effectively withdrawing the public company from the stock market and turning it into a privately owned one.

The purpose of privatization is to gain exclusive control of the stock, and therefore the company itself. Without an obligation to shareholders, and less oversight by the Securities and Futures Commission of Hong Kong, the sole proprietor of a privately owned company is empowered to make strategic business decisions on his or her own. For this reason, Li Ka-shing privatized the three listed companies affiliated with Cheung Kong. They included International Cities, Green Island Cement and Cavendish International.

Big shareholders hoping to take control generally buy stock from minority shareholders during so-called 'bear market' periods, when prices are low. This helps them save money, which amounts to making money.

Surprisingly, Li Ka-shing behaved differently in the process.

Privatization of International Cities was the first among the three, and it started in October 1985. But a year earlier, in 1984, with completion of the Sino-British Joint Declaration on Hong Kong's future, the Hong Kong stock market warmed up, and the stock index began to rise.

In this privatization, Li Ka-shing offered HK$1.01 for each share, 10% higher than the market price, which had already risen. Also, it was HK$0.01 higher than the company's IPO price. In this case, the small shareholders were overjoyed. They gladly sold to Li, and International Cities was privatized.

Li Ka-shing could have spent far less if he had chosen to privatize this company one or two years earlier. This had some people saying, "Superman is still a man, not a god. Li Ka-shing made a wrong decision the first time he privatized a company." Li heard this chatter, but he didn't take it seriously.

"We thought about that," he said, "but we believe that it is unfair for minority shareholders to sell out their stocks during a bear market."

It can be concluded that Li Ka-shing was a capable investor who didn't fail to find opportunities in the stock market. Yet, he took the interests of the minority shareholders into consideration. He'd rather spend more money than hurt those smaller investors who had followed and supported him since early on. Apart from his skill and wisdom in making money, this showed Superman Li's other approach to doing business.

In October 1988, Cheung Kong announced another privatization plan: for Green Island Cement. At that time, Cheung Kong owned 46% of the cement company. Li wanted to offer HK$20 per share to buy stock from minority shareholders. The market price was HK$17.7, which meant that Li Ka-shing again offered to pay 13% above the market price.

With such a generous buyout offer, which protected the minority shareholders' interests, this acquisition was completed by 30 December. Green Island Cement became a joint venture subsidiary and withdrew from public trading on the Hong Kong stock market.

The privatization of Cavendish International was more complex, and it went through many twists and turns. It had a far stronger financial base than International Cities or Green Island Cement. It was one of the four major listed companies in Cheung Kong's portfolio. Hutchison Whampoa had purchased the Hongkong Electric Company, Limited. Cavendish International was the non-electricity business of Hongkong Electric, developed by Simon Murray. When the company listed,

Hutchison Whampoa had 53.8% of its shares, and Cavendish International held 23%. Cavendish International's net asset value was HK$4.457 billion. In mid-1992, its market value was HK$15.509 billion.

In February 1991, Hutchison Whampoa announced that it would attempt to privatize Cavendish International. A total of HK$11.8 billion was spent on this acquisition, which was said to be one of the largest privatizations in the history of Hong Kong. Since Hutchison Whampoa already owned 65.28% of Cavendish International, the privatization could be done with no more than HK$0.41 billion.

Cavendish International pursued the acquisition because it had a limited ability to earn money, and its businesses overlapped with both Cheung Kong and Hutchison Whampoa. Hutchison Whampoa offered HK$4.1 per share, declaring that it would not go higher.

There was an evaluation of Cavendish International's assets, and it was believed that shares should be valued at HK$5-6. The current price of HK$4.1 would inevitably benefit the major shareholders and harm the interests of minor shareholders. Therefore, at the shareholders' meeting on 10 April, representatives for minor shareholders doubted the profitability of Cavendish International.

Cavendish International announced that it made a hefty profit of HK$1.316 billion in 1990 – 29% higher than the previous year – so its moneymaking abilities were not in question. At the same time, minority shareholders noted that the stock value of Hongkong Electric was rising every month. This would also lead to an increase in Cavendish International's turnover, which would promote its further development. That was why minority shareholders strongly opposed privatization. And so, with less than a quarter of shareholders supporting privatization, the acquisition drive came to an end.

Experts also believed that the purchase price was too low, and the acquirers' assessment of Cavendish International failed to reflect its actual performance. The purchase price was even far lower than the starting point of HK$4.3, when it was first listed in 1987. Li Ka-shing tended to pay much attention to the interests of minority shareholders, but in this purchase, it could be argued that he didn't show enough care for them, which ran contrary to Cheung Kong's operating style.

There were other underlying reasons for the failure of this privatization. For example, rumor had it that a British foundation tried to buy Cavendish International's stake. This showed that Cavendish International's stock was still attractive, and the price of HK$4.1 was too low. Simon Murray mistakenly claimed that they would not raise the price of the purchase, and he also ignored the feedback of the market, disappointing the minority shareholders.

What mattered the most was the sharp contrast between Cavendish International's good prospects and the tough terms faced by small shareholders. The reasons they didn't want to sell their stock were quite clear.

In accordance with the rules of the Securities and Futures Commission of Hong Kong, if a privatization effort failed, no proposal for privatization of the same company could be submitted for the following year.

Li Ka-shing learned a lesson, and spent time in deep discussion with Murray. They decided to submit another proposal to make Cavendish International private one year later, on 27 May 1992.

The new privatization drive was also led by Hutchison Whampoa. The offer price of HK$5.5 a share was 32% higher than their offer before the previous year's effort was suspended. At stake this time around was an asset valued at HK$5.838 billion. Li Ka-shing declared that this privatization was aimed at simplifying the internal structure of Cavendish International.

On 10 July, Cavendish International held a meeting of shareholders' representatives. The proposal for privatization was adopted, with 96.7% of the votes in favor of the sale, which was much higher than the number required. It could be said that the price was reasonable and the interests of both majority shareholders and smaller stock owners were protected.

In this privatization, Hutchison Whampoa bought 36.6% of the minority shareholders' shares at a price of HK$5.5. Overall, the deal cost HK$5.084 billion.

And with that, Cheung Kong had successfully completed three privatizations. It had preserved three listed companies on the Hong Kong exchange: Cheung Kong Property, Hutchison Whampoa and Hongkong Electric. The holding company's market value remained the greatest of any Hong Kong conglomerate.

Li Ka-shing had come far from his days as the 'King of Plastic Flowers.' After overcoming many setbacks, he became the richest person in Hong Kong, with real estate in one hand and stocks in the other. To generate profit was natural for a merchant, and that was certainly the case with Li Ka-shing. But how extraordinary it was that as he reaped profits for himself, Li tried to protect the interests of minority shareholders. This won people's sincere admiration. This balance is hard to achieve for many people, but Li could do it because of his passion and empathy.

From this perspective, 'Superman' was indeed a fitting moniker for Li Ka-shing.

The journey of life is destined to have its share of thorns. But Li Ka-shing always stayed calm and ended disputes in harmony. There were few people who behaved like him in the business world of Hong Kong or, for that matter, anywhere in the world.

CHAPTER 7

EXPANSION, PLANNING AND THE FUTURE

1. NEW AREAS

The Yangtze River rushed out of the Three Gorges, breaking forcefully through a bottleneck. The vast Jianghan Plain made it possible for the Yangtze to run across the territory. There was nothing that could rival its imposing manner and magnificent grace, let alone the grand scene in which the waterfowls beat their wings and flew to the sky.

At the end of the 1980s, after merging Hutchison Whampoa and acquiring Hongkong Electric, along with other privatizations, Cheung Kong Holdings ranked number one among all Hong Kong consortia. The name of 'Superman Li' was now known far and wide.

Companies under Cheung Kong advanced into many other areas beyond real estate. After the acquisition of Hongkong Electric, Li and Murray agreed that the most important commodity in the world was energy. Energy was an absolutely necessary part of people's lives. As a commodity, the market for energy was huge, and consumption was constantly growing. As a result, the sale of oil would certainly generate enormous fortunes.

But Hong Kong was a small peninsula with limited energy reserves. That was why Li Ka-shing looked for opportunities in distant North America. Specifically, he set his sights on Canada. With its vast territory, the country had abundant mineral and energy resources.

In past years, Li had moved into North America and forged alliances with both Canadian and US enterprises to sell plastic flowers. Importantly, his principles as a responsible businessman were admired by the Canadian Imperial Bank of Commerce.

In 1977, Li Ka-shing had invested in land and developed properties in Vancouver. In 1981, he invested a total of HK$70 billion to purchase port properties in Vancouver and Toronto. Another HK$60 billion was spent on buying the Toronto Hilton Hotel. In 1981, with the support of the Canadian bank, Li purchased the old site of the Vancouver World's Fair – 204 acres of land – for HK$3.2 billion.

Later, in 1988, together with Cheng Yu-tung, Chairman of New World Development of Hong Kong, and Lee Shau Kee, Chairman of Henderson Land Development Company, Li Ka-shing set up the Concord Pacific Company in Canada. Its focus was to renew the old World's Fair site, and to build Vancouver Concord Pacific Place, a huge residential development on the grounds of an abandoned railway yard.

All of this paled in comparison to Li's investment in Husky Energy, based in Calgary, in western Canada. His acquisition of the integrated energy company gave Li Ka-shing the most satisfaction. The profit and prestige it brought to Cheung Kong were beyond calculation.

In the past, light crude oil splashing from the ground put Saudi Arabia at the top of the world's wealth list overnight. Energy was a key to good fortune and brought wonderful changes to modern life. Oil is not only a fuel but also an important industrial material. From its role in transportation and building construction to clothing, oil is inextricably linked to people's lives, and as a commodity it is also unique.

But the market was quite strange. When there was increasing demand, supply rose. As a result, supply surpassed demand, the market became saturated and even the best product would be discounted.

Since the discovery of the best oil fields in the Middle East, large-scale exploration had sent crude oil to the energy market like an endless river. As a result, the price plummeted. The 1970s alone witnessed two oil price crises, and at its lowest the price hit $11 a barrel. Therefore, people were worried about the oil business.

It was against this background that Li Ka-shing came to Canada. With support from the Canadian Imperial Bank of Commerce, he made a play for Husky Energy. The president of Husky was Li Ka-shing's friend and this made his acquisition a transparent, altogether less troublesome, proposition.

In December 1986, assisted by Murray, Li bought 52% of Husky through Hutchison Whampoa for HK$3.2 billion.

The political environment was indeed unfavorable for the oil business. Political tensions mounted between Middle Eastern countries and the United States, and oil prices continued to drop. The Canadian oil company's performance became worse and worse. The oil prices were lower than the cost of extraction and processing, and this led to a heavy debt for the company. Li Ka-shing was ridiculed by his peers for the purchase. Most of Hong Kong's businessmen didn't appreciate his transnational investments, and they regarded this acquisition as a failure by Superman Li.

Had Li Ka-shing met his Waterloo?

In fact, the purchase decision was made after serious consideration. In his eyes, Canada was a very stable country, capable of resisting disturbances. Investment here would have fewer external risks. The falling of oil prices was only temporary, Li figured, because the automobile business and other global industries were bound to boom again, which would drive oil consumption and lead the price back to a reasonable level.

In addition to these external conditions, Cheung Kong's strength and leverage had been greatly enhanced through its operations in Hong Kong. Li started to seek opportunities overseas and to plan strategically for the company's further development. In view of the above conditions, Li Ka-shing made the decision to go against the trend.

Two years later, Li acquired another Canadian oil company and combined it with Husky. The assets of the restructured Husky doubled overnight. A few years later, after the withdrawal of another shareholder, Li once again increased his stake in the company. He now personally owned 30% of the shares, and together with Hutchison Whampoa's stake, he actually controlled more than 70% of the company. Therefore, Li Ka-shing enjoyed a controlling stake in Husky Energy, and this oil company became a large overseas subsidiary of Cheung Kong Holdings.

Li once described his acquisition of Husky in this way: "In the 1980s, the Middle East and the United States fell afoul of each other, and the oil supply was inadequate. At that time, Canada had huge oil reserves, and the political environment there was relatively stable, so I bought Husky when it was losing money."

In the years that followed, Husky would go on to bring him great profit. Superman Li was still human, of course, so he would naturally have felt proud.

Soon, the global situation stabilized, and the economy developed rapidly. As a result, the demand for oil grew, and oil prices rebounded. Under such circumstances, Husky made up the deficits and built up surpluses. It became a 'big cow' that regularly delivered 'milk' to Cheung Kong.

In 2000, Husky successfully carried out its initial public offering to raise funds. Though based in Canada, it invested in new energy sources around the world.

The shares personally held by Li Ka-shing alone generated dividends of nearly US$10 billion over the years. The overall dividends had already surpassed the amount of money he had originally invested, and Husky's market value reached US$30 billion. The shares held by Li had a market value of US$20 billion, which meant he had earned US$30 billion through stock value growth and dividends. This was the ultimate answer to the doubts about his investment in the Canadian energy company.

In the expansion of Cheung Kong Holdings, the acquisition of Hutchison Whampoa and Husky were milestones. They marked how the trickles of Cheung Kong gradually developed into a river. These decisions were not supported at the beginning, but they later proved to be effective choices. It was these choices that made Li Ka-shing and Cheung Kong Holdings what they are today. At the same time, the Husky acquisition also allowed Cheung Kong to delve into entirely new areas. It turned a Hong Kong consortium into a large multinational – a truly global enterprise.

As far as Chinese businessmen were concerned, Li Ka-shing had made a remarkable ascent from plastic flowers, to the real estate industry, then the stock market, and finally the energy field. He secured his crown of the richest Chinese person in the world.

Of course, the acquisition of Husky was not the end. Li Ka-shing was thinking about new strategies for the further development of his business empire.

2. ORANGE PLC

Everyone knew that 'Orange' was an English name.

In the 1990s, it was a telecommunications company launched by Hutchison Whampoa in the UK, mainly providing mobile telephone services. This British telecom company had a small market share and limited profitability under the management of Simon Murray. It was one of Murray's less successful endeavors, unfolding as he was about to leave Hutchison Whampoa.

Murray left office in 1993, and was succeeded by Canning Fok. Canning is a figure who warrants a detailed introduction. He played an important role in the development of Cheung Kong. According to Li Ka-shing, he was seen as a shrewd man, full of ideas for making money.

Canning was born in Hong Kong in 1951. He graduated from St John's University in Minnesota and qualified there as a professional accountant. When he returned to Hong Kong in 1979, Li Ka-shing hired him to work for Cheung Kong, taking charge of the financial affairs. That marked the beginning of his long and successful career.

After that, he went to study at the University of New England in Australia and was qualified as an Australian accountant. He was promoted to Executive Director of Hutchison Whampoa in 1984, and named Vice Director and General Manager in 1987. In 1993, he formally took over as the Director and General Manager, which made him a competent assistant to Li Ka-shing and gave him significant power in the company.

Canning was 'a professional manager,' meaning he had no direct relationship with capital and was a pure wage earner. But the position he had as an employee was much higher than other workers, since he could direct the daily operation of the whole enterprise.

How outstanding was Canning? Some praised him as the 'emperor among workers.' With this position, he was naturally the employee who was paid the most. His annual salary was HK$124 million, which was an amazing figure at that time. Such a legendary figure certainly racked up incredible achievements. Otherwise, why would Li Ka-shing, the shrewdest of businessmen, pay him such an astronomical salary?

The sale of Orange in Britain was Canning's main contribution to Cheung Kong. Orange operated poorly in the UK and accounted for only a small share of the UK telecom market. Most people instead chose the German telecom giant Mannesmann or UK's Vodafone LSE for mobile services.

After taking office, Canning made every effort to attract public attention and even invested another US$500 million to expand Orange's business in the UK market. It gradually gained a firmer foothold. Vodafone and Mannesmann dominated the communication services market in Europe, followed by Orange as the third largest provider. But the gap between the two leaders and the third-place contender was a wide one.

Vodafone was determined to be the leader of the global communications industry, and its stumbling block was Mannesmann. This competition between the two was like the old Chinese fable of the fight between the clam and the snipe, in which a fisherman comes along and catches them both. Although Orange was small, it could find its own space and achieve its development between the two bigger rivals.

At that time, Vodafone President Christopher Gent was ambitious; he wanted to be a pioneer in the telecommunication industry. Under his leadership, Vodafone expanded rapidly, operating in 25 countries and regions. It even held the highest market share in Japan. Facing Vodafone's unbridled expansion, Mannesmann was inevitably worried.

Although there was an invisible agreement between the two that they had their clearly divided markets in Europe,

Mannesmann still felt threatened by Vodafone's aggressiveness. In order to survive and develop, Mannesmann turned to Britain, and Li Ka-shing's Orange.

Li was very clear that Orange was no match for Vodafone. Especially at a time when Hong Kong was struck in an economic crisis, he could not concentrate on the European market. Although Orange ranked third in Britain, it in fact had a very small market share in the UK, unlike the huge Vodafone.

However, Li Ka-shing's shrewdness and Canning's business strategies could be of great use. Instead of handing over Orange to Vodafone, they contacted Mannesmann.

Mannesmann was planning to buy Orange because it was the only fortress on the way to Britain. Anyone who bought it could take advantage of that situation and enter the UK. Although its market share was small, it was strategically positioned geographically. And with that, it would be possible for Mannesmann or Vodafone to make greater strides. Mannesmann also showed its willingness to merge with Orange.

Li Ka-shing dispatched Canning to London to manage Orange's operations and negotiate with Mannesmann privately.

Britain and Germany, facing each other across the sea, were known for their incessant feuding, and they had battled each other through the centuries. Even when the two countries met at a football match, the game was particularly ferocious. As a result, as Canning was negotiating with Mannesmann in London, the news of their cooperative intention reached Vodafone. The German telecom company certainly didn't want to give up this wonderful opportunity, because to conquer Orange was the prerequisite for entering the British market.

However, at this point the initiative was firmly in the hands of Li and Canning. After rounds of dramatic negotiations, Orange fell to Mannesmann. This acquisition also greatly benefited Li and Hutchison Whampoa, which received US$2.8 billion in cash and an additional US$2.8 billion in notes that would be paid over three years. At the same time, because Mannesmann paid Li with some of its shares, Li also received 10% of Mannesmann's stock after its integration of Orange. In other words, he obtained 52 million shares of Mannesmann.

And with that, Li Ka-shing's personal assets jumped by HK$15 billion.

There were certainly many stories behind such a big deal, and the main reason for the high selling price was the competition between Vodafone and Mannesmann. Part of this came from the 10% stake Li gained in Mannesmann. With his new stake in the company, Li Ka-shing appointed Canning to both Mannesmann's Board of Directors and its senior Advisory Panel.

But the story didn't end there. The ambitious Vodafone couldn't accept such an outcome. As the Chinese saying goes: 'How can a man allow others to sleep soundly near his own bed?'

Soon, Vodafone proposed a £68 billion plan to fully acquire Mannesmann. This was a huge temptation for all, since Mannesmann could never otherwise command such a high price. However, the offer was rejected by Mannesmann immediately. Just five days later, Vodafone's negotiator told Mannesmann that the revised offer was £79 billion.

Mannesmann was the largest mobile phone operator in Germany, with 17 million customers. After the acquisition of Orange, its customer base reached 20 million.

Behind it was also one of the oldest consortia in Germany, with more than a century of history. For this reason, the Germans claimed that they had deep feelings for the company and did not want it to leave Germany. As a result, the £79 billion offer was also rejected several days later.

Incredibly, Vodafone was not going to give up. It offered an even higher price of £105 billion, or US$185 billion. A large amount of money like this was all but irresistible. And Mannesmann's shareholders had to have been tempted. Moreover, Mannesmann was a listed company – it was publicly traded, and 60% of its shareholders were not German. They deemed the affection of the Germans useless, so they announced that they would give up Mannesmann and sell it to the British.

Tens of thousands of German people took to the streets to protest the sale, which some senior government officials were now calling a hostile takeover.

However, Germany was a country of free capitalism. Shareholders, as the owners of publicly traded companies, were those companies' owners. Their decisions were protected by the law. Therefore, with the temptation of £105 billion, the majority of Mannesmann's shareholders decided to sell.

On 13 November 1999, Mannesmann was successfully acquired by Vodafone. Li Ka-shing's shares in Mannesmann were also sold, bringing him more than HK$50 billion.

3. RETAIL INDUSTRY

Some media described Li Ka-shing's successful operation in the UK as "Superman picking up a sweet orange in Europe." Through this buying in and selling out, he had earned more than HK$100 billion. This orange was sweet indeed!

Meanwhile, Cheung Kong's shareholders benefited from the success of Hutchison Whampoa. Cheung Kong also performed well in the stock markets in Hong Kong and London.

This reflected people's approval of Cheung Kong as well as Li Ka-shing. Their wisdom in the ways of business also made Li and Canning increasingly famous.

Li then expanded his focus on the energy sector, getting into oil in the South China Sea and natural gas in Australia.

It was amazing that as Li's business empire spread all over the world, its closest association with ordinary people was the retail space, through a chain of stores called AS Watson.

Watsons was a century-old British company that began as the Canton Dispensary and Soda Water Establishment, in Guangdong. It moved to Hong Kong and was rebranded AS Watson & Company in 1871. Since Watsons in Cantonese was pronounced 'Quchen,' the store was pronounced 'Quchenshi' in Mandarin. By the late 19th century, the Watsons chain had more than 30 stores in Hong Kong, mainly selling cosmetics and daily necessities.

In the 1960s, Watsons was acquired by Hutchison Whampoa. Later, when Li Ka-shing bought Hutchison Whampoa, Watsons naturally became part of Cheung Kong. It soon expanded worldwide, along with the global development of Cheung Kong. That expansion ramped up when Cheung Kong entered mainland China, with Watsons stores opening one after another, serving hundreds of millions of customers every day.

The scope of its business was expanded from cosmetics and daily necessities to encompass healthcare, food, electronics and fine wines. It also produced beverages such as bottled water, juice, soda and tea drinks. Through international wine wholesalers and agents, it stocked the world's best wines, and its stores opened at airports and ports.

High volume sales at Watsons made some brands world famous. It made a higher quality of life possible for its consumers, and also made Watsons a world-renowned name.

Watsons sought to provide products and services tailored to the needs of its customers, at the most affordable prices. Its stores were known for their fine-quality products and the hospitality of staff. They valued regional markets' unique needs and wants, and launched a wide range of product combinations based on those market preferences.

Watsons struck a good balance between market expansion and meeting local needs in developing its international business, and this unique style set it apart from the world's major retailers.

In Asia, Watsons owned several well-known brands and retail chains, including Watsons Personal Care Store, PARKnSHOP, and other food and retail outlets. There were also Watsons Wine stores and airport retail chains. It was a major manufacturer of local bottled water and other beverages. That its 'Watsons Water' was the bestseller among all the bottled waters in Hong Kong reflects the market acceptance of the company's products. In Europe, Watsons retail business spread to 26 countries and many of its brands had outstanding performance in the market.

Li Ka-shing never forgot that it was a century-old enterprise. Under his guidance, Watsons successfully entered Europe. In 2005, Li decided to invest HK$5.5 billion to merge Watsons with France's largest perfume retailer, Marionnaud. This was Watson's first expansion into Europe, setting the stage for expansion across the rest of the continent.

As a whole, Europe was prosperous, and Watsons suited its large, stable middle-class. This acquisition brought another 1,300 chain stores into the Watsons fold and increased its financial assets by HK$10 billion.

In the same year, Li Ka-shing acquired the Spektr-Group, a health and beauty products chain in St Petersburg, Russia. This expansion consolidated its position as the world's largest retailer in the personal care, beauty and skincare industry. Watsons also successfully completed several acquisitions in the UK and the Netherlands, further expanding its business in Europe.

In 2003, Watsons acquired a well-known pharmaceutical retailer in the Philippines and expanded its business to Southeast Asia. In 2004, it completed the successful acquisition of the biggest beauty and skin care retailer in Latvia and Lithuania, providing entry to the Baltic countries.

Through mergers and acquisitions, Li Ka-shing also expanded Watsons operating scale in key areas of Asia and Europe, marketing the lifestyle notion of 'health, beauty, happiness.' It would help those who loved life, and pursued a good quality of life, to achieve unity in their internal and external beauty. It actually introduced the concept of 'personal care' in many places and gained great traction with young women.

It also paid attention to the development of its own brands. There were more than 1,200 kinds of shower gels and shampoos sold by Watsons, accounting for 15% of its sales. The development of these brands was based on its market research. In order to make the goods marketable, a simulated store would be established to identify sales trends and determine customer needs, making it easier to decide what types of products should be promoted. They also launched many products with special features to meet the needs of specific consumer segments.

For example, Watsons solved some problems women experienced wearing fashionable shoes. They invented stickers to buffer the friction between feet and high heels.

Since the spirit of the enterprise was shown in details, Watsons' customer-oriented service made it the eminent pioneer in the retailing industry. After Watsons entered mainland China, it continued to expand and won the favor of many domestic consumers.

Let's look at the development of Watsons, the Chinese retail giant, in the Chinese market:

- In 1989, China's first Watsons personal care store opened in Beijing
- In 1994, Watsons returned to Guangzhou and was located on Jiangnan West Road
- In 2005, Watsons' 100th branch store opened in Guangzhou Zhengjia Plaza
- In 2006, the 200th store in mainland China opened in Huadu, Guangzhou
- In 2007, the 300th mainland Chinese location opened in Nanjing, Jiangsu
- In 2008, the 400th mainland Watsons opened in Haikou, Hainan
- In 2009, the 500th mainland outlet opened in Shanghai
- In 2010, the 600th Watsons in mainland China opened in Shenzhen
- In 2011, the 1,000th store in mainland China opened in Shanghai – the 10,000th store in the world
- In 2013, the 1,500th store in mainland China opened in Anhui

- In 2014, the 2,000[th] mainland store opened in Tianjin
- In 2015, the 12,000[th] Watsons location opened in Hong Kong, as the chain's global flagship store

Currently, Watsons has branches and affiliates in 24 countries. With more than 14,400 stores, it is one of the world's largest chain retailers.

Now, the subsidiary of Hutchison Whampoa has annual revenues of HK$135 billion. On average, the company can earn 300 million yuan per day. Just in this sector, there are 100,000 employees working for Li Ka-shing. The chain serves four billion people per year, and few e-commerce platforms are comparable in this aspect.

Every enterprise has its own culture, and the boss's personal style is bound to have a big influence on it. Watsons not only has its own unique brand, but also its own distinctive approach to service. It is based on the customer's actual needs, and this reflects the culture of the company.

As the old saying goes, 'The Yangtze River does not reject a trickle, so it can flow a 1,000 li.' Li's operation truly brings this analogy to life.

4. THE BUSINESS EMPIRE

As previously mentioned, Li Ka-shing built his business empire gradually, from Cheung Kong Plastic Factory into Cheung Kong Industries, and then into Cheung Kong Holdings. He expanded his territory from Shau Kei Wan to North Point, then to Central Queen's Road. He also successfully expanded his business from Hong Kong to Europe, North America, and even as far as Australia, Singapore and Southeast Asia.

In the process, he explored a wide range of industries and built his business empire with honesty, credibility, business acumen, an imposing manner and flexible investment strategies. As of 2014, the total market capitalization of Cheung Kong Holdings in Hong Kong was HK$1,054 billion, and it operated in 52 countries with over 280,000 employees.

Li Ka-shing devoted his life to piecing together this powerful consortium, a staggeringly huge enterprise with hundreds of thousands of workers.

Let's look back at the expansion of this empire, and detail further developments we have not mentioned before.

Li Ka-shing was born in 1928, in Chaozhou, Guangdong. In order to avoid the chaos of World War II and earn a living for his family after the death of his father, the teenage Li started as an apprentice in a teahouse. He also learned clock repair and took on peddling buckets before joining the plastic factory where he worked his way up from salesman to manager.

In 1950, when Li was only 22 years old, he founded Cheung Kong Plastic Factory. Later, it was renamed Cheung Kong Industrial Company, Limited, although it remained focused on manufacturing plastic. It could be seen from this name that Li Ka-shing had the ambition to recruit talents and absorb funds for his company in the integrative style of the Yangtze River. He wanted to build his company into an inclusive enterprise from very early on.

In 1957, Li Ka-shing saw in an English magazine that a plastic factory in Italy had successfully invented colorful plastic flowers. They had the same color and lustre as real-life flowers and could be kept indefinitely. He immediately realized that this would be a key product that the market needed. This predictive sense – of what will be the next big thing – is important in a business of any sort. Without it, Li's dream could only ever have been a dream. Luckily, he was aware of it and flew to Italy to learn the skills and technology.

After returning to Hong Kong, his advanced technology and excellent business strategies earned him his claim to fame as the 'King of Plastic Flowers.' His dream to build Cheung Kong into an inclusive enterprise was finally achieved.

In 1958, Li Ka-shing built his first office building in Hong Kong's North Point district, marking his entry into the real estate field. In 1960, his second building was erected in the Chai Wan neighborhood, and Li started to focus on property.

Soon after, land prices in Hong Kong plummeted, and Li Ka-shing decisively bought a number of lots, which later provided sufficient land resources for the development of Cheung Kong. God blessed him with the valuable opportunity, which he grasped with perfect timing. The land brought him incalculable assets, which made his dream of the Yangtze River shine more brightly.

In 1972, Cheung Kong Holdings Company, Limited, was listed on the main board of the Hong Kong Stock Exchange. This was another milestone in its history. Li Ka-shing grew his operation in an imposing manner on the stock market. He absorbed funds, merged companies and created one miracle after another.

In 1979, he acquired Hutchison Whampoa. For Li and his Cheung Kong industries, this was an epoch-making event.

Hutchison used to be a British-owned company. During World War II, an Englishman named Sir Douglas Clague was dispatched to Hong Kong for military service, after fighting through India, Burma and Thailand. At the end of the war, he went to work for Hutchison in Hong Kong, and after a series of promotions became its Chairman. The company acquired Watsons, Dak Wai Bou, Whampoa Dock and other businesses, which greatly expanded its scale and reach. In 1969, Clague entered the real estate industry and was once the biggest landlord in Hong Kong.

In 1975, the expansion of Hutchison encountered a headwind. The stock market plummeted, the oil market was in crisis and the company experienced financial problems. The situation worsened due to the sharp depreciation of stock. The expiration of loans left no way of escape for Hutchison. Finally, it agreed to have HSBC buy 33.65% of its shares, and HSBC became its largest shareholder. Clague had to step down, and was no longer in charge of Hutchison.

In 1977, HSBC merged Hutchison and Whampoa, and the new company was named Hutchison Whampoa Company, Limited. It was listed in 1978, underwritten by HSBC.

Li Ka-shing once again seized a golden opportunity. With the help of Yue-Kong Pao and Michael Sandberg, he easily acquired Hutchison Whampoa. With a 22.4% ownership stake, he became a board member and later Chairman, taking full control of the company. This made his Cheung Kong Holdings renowned overnight in Hong Kong.

In 1973, Cheung Kong Holdings acquired PARKnSHOP.

In 1977, it bought the Hilton Hotel and its shopping centre in Hong Kong, which later was developed into Cheung Kong Holdings' business centre.

In 1980, Cheung Kong extracted the management and business resources of Hutchison Whampoa and established the Hutchison Whampoa Real Estate Group.

In 1983, Hutchison Whampoa launched a mobile phone service in Hong Kong.

In 1985, Cheung Kong acquired the Hongkong Electric Company, Limited, through Hutchison Whampoa. The Chinese name of Hongkong Electric was changed but the English version remained the same.

In 1987, Li acquired 43% of Husky Energy in Canada, through Hutchison Whampoa, and its business expanded overseas in the field of energy.

In 1996, Hutchison Whampoa integrated the marketing and operational resources of mobile, paging and fixed networks in Hong Kong, and set up a new company named Hutchison Telecommunications, Limited.

In 1997, Cheung Kong industries carried out a large-scale restructuring. After that, Cheung Kong's stake in Hutchison Whampoa rose to 48.95%. Hutchison Whampoa controlled 84.58% of Cheung Kong Infrastructure Holdings' shares. Hutchison Whampoa also ceded 35.01% of Hongkong Electric's stake to Cheung Kong Infrastructure Holdings.

In 1998, with investment by Cheung Kong, 'The Centre' was completed as a Hong Kong landmark. In the same year, the company also invested in agricultural industries in mainland China and entered the hotel business there through Harbour Plaza Hotels.

In 1999, the 70-storey Cheung Kong Holdings headquarters, the Cheung Kong Centre, was constructed in the heart of central Hong Kong.

In 2004, the Beijing Oriental Plaza was completed. With a total area of 763,482 square metres, it included shopping malls, office buildings, serviced apartments and hotels.

By 2014, Cheung Kong's business had expanded worldwide, making it a truly multinational enterprise. Its businesses spanned property, real estate agencies and management, ports and related services, telecommunications, hotels, retail, energy, infrastructure, finance and investment, e-commerce, building materials, media, life-sciences technology and much more.

At this point, Li Ka-shing's dream was fully realized, and his Cheung Kong, with its great vitality, became the envy of the world.

Li devoted his life to his business empire and became the richest man in contemporary China.

His life experiences always filled people with mixed feelings. He was just a weak, dispossessed little boy when he first left his small village in Chaozhou. But he didn't yield to hardship and disappear; he stubbornly survived by his own effort. With great ambition, he started from the basics in each field he entered, learning step by step. With a wonderful control of the rhythm of his life, he wasted no opportunity and headed for his bright future.

It was not sheer luck that brought about Li Ka-shing's success. Good fortune might have favored him once or twice, but he could not depend on it all the time. It was his personality, life experiences, characteristics, inspiration and the decisiveness at crucial moments that helped him to achieve his success.

And it was his admiration for the Yangtze River that was the origin of all his successes. Without this long-lasting admiration and the ambitious dream, Li could never have built his business empire.

CHAPTER

DREAMS, INHERITANCE AND COMPASSION

1. LI KA-SHING'S WIFE

We've said that luck was not what brought Li Ka-shing his great success, but in terms of investment and accumulating wealth in the business world, he did have his share of luck. He seldom lost, even in the unpredictable stock market.

However, his personal life was not blessed. It was widely held in China that losing one's mother at an early age and losing one's wife in middle age were among the greatest tragedies in a person's life. Li Ka-shing's mother acted as an excellent mentor in his family life, but Li lost his father when he was young. The lack of a father's love burdened him with the hardship of life too early.

Later, he married his cousin, Chong Yuet Ming. Her name in Chinese referred to the bright moon, and she was just as beautiful and gentle as the moon. More importantly, her mind was bright and pure. She held innocent love for her cousin Li Ka-shing, who once fell on evil days.

Despite her father's strong opposition, and the fact that she had received a far better education than Li, Chong Yuet Ming's love for him was consistent. This love itself could be written down as another legend.

It all came to an abrupt end on 1 January 1990, when Chong Yuet Ming died at the age of 58, when Li Ka-shing was 62 years old.

The death of Chong Yuet Ming did not have much impact on Cheung Kong. Since the birth of Li Ka-shing's two sons, Chong Yuet Ming mainly spent her time caring for the children and attended few public events. But Chong's death had a great impact on Li's personal life, Of course, outsiders could hardly understand his pain, but Li Ka-shing did not marry again.

On the first day of every year – the anniversary of his wife's death – Li would show up in the Buddhist cemetery in Chai Wan, Hong Kong. Whether it was sunny, gloomy or rainy on that day, he would bring his family to visit and sweep Chong Yuet Ming's tomb.

Journalists and businessmen waited in the cemetery for his arrival, and as soon as he appeared for this solemn duty, a crowd would gather around him. Reporters wanted to seize the chance for an interview, and businessmen came seeking investment in their projects. Time never stops and no one can escape the natural ageing process. Li Ka-shing's physical condition was declining and his will wavered. However, his affection for his wife never diminished.

Li announced his decision to retire on 16 March 2018, when he was 90. At that time, the media reported his mourning routine, nearly three decades after the death of his wife:

"Although Li Ka-shing is a billionaire, he has never forgotten his wife. In the past 29 years, his whole family has mourned for Chong Yuet Ming at the anniversary of her death. Li Ka-shing is much thinner than before. His back seems quite weak and has stooped a bit. Even with his children's help, he still walks laboriously. But his face still shows that he is an energetic person. People were worried about his physical condition, but he is in much better shape than before. He relied on crutches to walk when he was in his 70s and 80s, but now he can walk by himself, though he cannot stand up straight."

The business world is emotion-free, because sentiment makes people weak and dependent, which will lead to indecisiveness and then big mistakes. But in life, if someone has no feelings, people despise him for being so vegetation-like.

Li Ka-shing's assets were worth billions of dollars, but he still cherished his wife. Because of this contrast, the true feelings shown by Li seemed more valuable. Once a list of successful Chinese businessmen was made, regarding how much they cherished affection, and Superman Li was among the top three.

2. VICTOR LI, THE ELDEST SON

Li Ka-shing had a famous saying: "No matter how successful a person is in his career, to neglect his children's education cannot be forgiven."

On 1 August 1964, Li Ka-shing's eldest son, Victor Li, was born. Going forwards, Chong Yuet Ming made it her responsibility to provide an educational environment at home. As a mother, she was gentle and knowledgeable. Her words and deeds greatly influenced Victor Li from his earliest days.

Li, who came from a poor family and rose through various hardships, always felt that superior family background was not necessarily conducive to the growth of his son. Therefore, aside from providing an excellent education, he disciplined Victor strictly, and the boy was never spoiled.

Victor finished his primary and secondary education at St Paul's English College in Hong Kong. In terms of high school education, Li Ka-shing arranged for him to study in Canada for three years. Li only covered the necessary living expenses during this period; all other costs were paid by Victor himself.

When Victor left Hong Kong, he was almost the same age as his father had been when he began his apprenticeship at the teahouse. He bore in mind all his father's teachings and never made any extravagant purchases or demands.

He lived far from his family, and gradually developed the ability to live independently.

After graduating from high school, Victor was admitted to Stanford University in America. At his father's request, he majored in civil engineering, as Li Ka-shing believed that real estate was the foundation of Cheung Kong. Perhaps he already knew at that time that he wanted Victor to take over Cheung Kong one day.

In the mid-1980s, Victor received his PhD in structural engineering from Stanford and returned to Hong Kong.

The return of Victor Li caused a great stir in Cheung Kong Holdings. Despite being in the spotlight, the young man joined the company like an ordinary employee, serving as a clerk in the headquarters, with routine responsibilities.

Some executives asked Li Ka-shing why he had not let his son join the board of directors. Since Cheung Kong was Li's company, it would have been totally acceptable for Victor, the eldest son, to sit on the board. Li rejected this suggestion, perhaps fearful that Victor might take this privilege for granted. He wanted his son to start as an employee like any other and gain knowledge about everything in the company.

To start as an ordinary employee was only one step in the normal treatment Victor received. Li Ka-shing's plans for training Victor Li were anything but relaxed. He arranged for George Magnus to be Victor's mentor, to teach him how to do business. Magnus had graduated from Cambridge University's Department of Economics and had worked as a senior expert in the business world. As Vice Chairman of the Board of Directors of Cheung Kong Holdings, he was in fact the second in command.

As the saying goes, great teachers always have brilliant students. Magnus said this of his protégé: "Victor is a great young man who is modest and studious. He doesn't behave like a son of a world-class tycoon at all."

While Victor was still studying in Canada, Li moved him into a key part of his business in that country. In 1986, under Li's leadership, Cheung Kong's leaders marched into the market of North America and Europe. Li, Simon Murray and Magnus often held business talks with Canadian officials and businessmen. Victor frequently appeared in those meetings, but he never said much. He just observed the others' actions and privately absorbed the essence of the discussions.

In December 1986, after Li Ka-shing paid HK$3.2 billion to buy a 52% stake in Canada's Husky Energy, Victor started to take care of his family's business in Canada. This was the first time his father tasked Victor with being a 'local leader.'

This time Li commented on Victor's success. "If you are in Hong Kong, this will be big news," he said. "Even if you hide in the bedroom of the hotel, you will be harassed by phone calls from the media."

This was overheard by Husky employees and reported to the company's chairman, Akash Bhullar. He immediately held a grand banquet for Li and his son, inviting dignitaries from Canada's political and business circles. Under the spotlight, Victor appeared with a bright smile. Everyone knew that this was Li Ka-shing's eldest child and they were clear about his mission.

At that moment, for the first time, Li Ka-shing's intention to step back a little was evident.

Victor's performance in Canada did not disappoint his father. He became famous in his first competitive business engagement, which impressed everyone in Cheung Kong Holdings. It was a development project on the old 1986 World's Fair site in Vancouver.

After the fair, temporary exhibition halls for all countries were either demolished or abandoned, making the site a very desolate place. It was situated on a narrow strip of land near the sea.

Victor, who had studied civil engineering, was optimistic about the land and believed it could be transformed into a successful commercial development. Away from the hustle and bustle of the city, facing the sea, he was convinced that this different setting would attract many people, drawn by the quietness and leisure of the place.

This deserted piece of land, far from the downtown area, was public property, owned by the provincial government. The price would be low if anyone decided to buy it.

Victor was not acting on a whim. He evaluated the land from a professional perspective and put forwards to his father five reasons why they should acquire it.

First, the area around the World's Fair site had been developed, and the community and transportation facilities had already been established. Second, Vancouver was different from other large cities. There was no elevated freeway, which ensured beautiful views of the Pacific Coast scenery. Third, it was located at the edge of the urban area, so it enjoyed the advantages of the suburbs, was free from the disadvantages of the urban area, and was convenient for residents to commute between the city and the suburbs. Fourth, situated near the sea, the development would offer a pleasant view, and it would certainly command handsome tenant prices because of this. Finally, the migration of Hong Kong residents to Canada continued to increase in droves. The people of Hong Kong suffered from noise and congestion in the urban areas, but they felt it was too remote and lonely to live in that city's suburbs.

Li Ka-shing appreciated this proposal, especially for the last reason. He thought that Victor not only understood civil engineering, but also the real estate market. He had business acumen.

However, the piece of land was too large, equivalent to the entire Chai Wan district plus Causeway Bay. Such a large-scale project would not only have been unprecedented in Hong Kong, but unparalleled in Canada. But Li Ka-shing was a pioneer. He immediately invited Hong Kong's other real estate giants, Lee Shau Kee and Cheng Yu-tung, to join the project, together with Concorde Company, a subsidiary of the Canadian Imperial Commercial Bank.

The person in charge of this project was Victor Li.

Such an undertaking was a huge challenge for someone as young as Victor, but he lived up to the expectations of his father and the other principles. He worked day and night to push the development forwards.

In his book, *The Rich Second Generation*, author Xiao Liang Sheng offered these observations:

"For this grand plan, Victor Li masterminded and designed it all by himself. He devoted endless efforts to it. Over two years he attended more than 200 public hearings, be they large or small, and met more than 20,000 people from all walks of life to publicize the plan. Of course, his father, teachers and other people gave him unlimited support."

Some extremely prejudiced media reports aroused resentment among local residents, who printed leaflets and appealed to the provincial government to stop development of the site.

Victor Li immediately made an appointment with David See-chai Lam, Governor of the Canadian province of British Columbia, where Vancouver is located. He asked, "Do you know what it would mean to suspend the project?"

The young man's calm demeanor and direct question shocked Lam, and because the governor was also a Hong Kong immigrant, he fully understood what Victor meant. The province would lag behind if the real estate investment flowing into it was reduced by 2/3.

Lam hastened to explain to the Canadian Parliament, while Victor successfully persuaded the public with his excellent delivery and rationale.

Soon after the disturbance was settled, the Concord Pacific Place project was completed. The *Hong Kong Economic Journal* published a special report, "Victor Li's Design of Concord Pacific Place, Surprise to the Whole World." It said the following:

"For Victor Li, the Concord Pacific project was the touchstone of his career. He masterminded this construction project, which was the largest in Canada's history. He took part in everything from site selection to land purchase, development and publicity. He devoted all his energy to it. From the purchase to the construction, he encountered countless disputes, accidents and difficulties. If a person with weak will and insufficient confidence faced this, he would have already cowered, but Victor did not behave in that way. He worked meticulously, ignoring praise and criticism from the outside. The more he fought, the braver he became. Eventually, he succeeded."

Li Ka-shing saw this and rejoiced over it. After the completion of the Concord Pacific Place, he promoted Victor to the board of Cheung Kong Holdings at the request of other board members.

In October 1992, Li Ka-shing stepped back and passed his seat on the Hong Kong General Chamber of Commerce to Victor, making him the youngest member of the group.

In April 1992, Li resigned as Non-Executive Vice Chairman of HSBC, and Victor joined the bank's board of directors.

Finally, in February 1993, Cheung Kong Holdings' board announced that it was promoting Victor to the position of Deputy Director and General Manager, situating him just below George Magnus.

Li Ka-shing had long warned his son, "Always keep a low profile." Victor followed that advice. When he and his girlfriend Wong Fu-seon got married, there were only ten tables at the banquet. (Victor's brother, Richard Li, was playing video games in the VIP room.) This low-key event stunned many relatives and friends, who heard the news afterwards and came to congratulate them.

3. RICHARD LI, THE SECOND SON

Some people called Richard Li a lone ranger.

Richard was born in November 1966. Two years younger than Victor, he was seldom alone. At home, he had his mother's care. Outside, Li Ka-shing had a socialization routine in place since Richard's childhood.

From the age of 10, he and Victor attended the Cheung Kong Holdings' Board of Directors meetings. The children were so small that they could barely see what was going on around the conference room table. They looked around with curiosity while others debated. This special sight showed how Li Ka-shing loved his sons and how he tried to expose them to the business environment from an early age, which would help them accomplish great things in the future.

Richard himself said that his father never talked about how to do business, but taught his boys 'how to be a real man.' The standards his father passed on were extracted from the teachings of Confucius and Mencius.

Before he was 14 years old, Richard was sent to North America to attend a college preparatory school. Every student there, rich or poor, had a strong sense of independence. Richard soon got used to this way of life.

Once, when Li Ka-shing went to visit his son, he was told that Richard was on the tennis court. He found that Richard was actually picking up balls for others. He was doing so to earn a little extra money to cover his living expenses. This made Li overjoyed. When he returned to Hong Kong, he praised his son repeatedly to Chong Yuet Ming – Richard had learned to work while studying, and he would surely achieve great things in the future. His love for his sons was beyond words.

At the age of 17, Richard was admitted to Stanford University, majoring in his favorite subject: computer engineering. It seemed that this was by no means Li Ka-shing's choice. Li could have asked him to study business or law, which would have been useful in managing the family business empire and complemented his brother Victor's education and professional role. But this was Richard's own choice, and his father respected it.

In 1987, the 21-year-old Richard Li graduated from university. Li Ka-shing's interests in Canada were booming, and Richard moved there, but he did not manage the business like his brother did. Instead, he went to work at a bank, as an ordinary employee, and became a real contributor in the IT department. These two choices were obviously not aligned with the family business, and they seemed to be the lone ranger's personal choices. This showed Richard's personality, as well as Li Ka-shing's love for him.

Four years later, Richard returned to Hong Kong. It was not clear whether this was his own choice or his father's will.

However, Li Ka-shing immediately arranged for him to join Hutchison Whampoa, where he learned under the CEO, Simon Murray. After talking with him, Murray assigned Richard to Hutchison Telecommunications, as an ordinary employee, in a position where he could work with computers.

Richard Li quickly focused on satellite TV. No one knew whether he had planned this for a long time or not, but this definitely interested Richard. So, why did he choose satellite TV?

On 24 February 1988, at Li Ka-shing's initiative, Asia-Sat, a joint venture between Hutchison Whampoa, CITIC and Taai Dung, was established. It was to invest in launching a satellite that would provide telecommunication services in Asia. The group planned to use the Chinese Long March 3 series launch vehicle (CZ-3) to send the satellite into geosynchronous orbit over Southeast Asia.

The satellite was named AsiaSat 1, and it was successfully launched on 7 April 1990. Its original purpose was to provide telephone services, which would be operated by Hutchison Telecommunications, where Richard Li now worked. The satellite had a total of 24 transponders, with annual rent of about US$25 million, but they were rarely used. Therefore, Li and Richard decided to make full use of their satellite in the field of satellite TV.

Hong Kong is a tiny place. There were originally two TV stations, Hongkong TV (TVB) and Asia Television Limited (ATV). These two stations earned profits from their advertisements. Later, cable TV was developed, and the Hong Kong government set up a second telecommunications network for the convenience of management. Users of cable TV would be charged for the service, which was quite different from how traditional TV broadcasting over the public airwaves worked.

Li Ka-shing wanted to invest in this new broadcasting system, but someone else grabbed the opportunity first. Who was this person? Peter Woo, Chairman of the Board of WTT HK Limited and son-in-law of Yue-Kong Pao, who ran the world's largest shipping fleet. Like Richard Li, Woo was also young and had strong support.

After losing out on the big cable TV opportunity, Li Ka-shing wanted to reset with the development of satellite TV, with Richard heading up the effort. Simon Murray soon appointed Richard Director and Chief Executive of the satellite TV business. With Cheung Kong's own satellite, there seemingly would be no competition.

In fact, it would not be so easy. There was an issue of regulatory permission. And wireless technology infrastructure would only support a limited number of channels.

Satellite TV was also a kind of wireless TV. To receive signals from a satellite, a special satellite dish must be installed on a residence. Statistics showed that satellite dishes could be installed on 150,000 buildings in Hong Kong.

In August 1990, Li Ka-shing lobbied hard and finally persuaded the Hong Kong government to relax the relevant rules. The new regulations stipulated that people who used satellite dishes to receive satellite TV signals didn't need to apply for any approval or license, as long as the equipment was not commercial in nature (charging the users) or used for re-broadcasting (charging wireless stations and cable stations for customer access services).

In this way, satellite TV posed a great threat to cable TV. Immediately, Peter Woo prohibited companies qualified to install satellite dishes from entering buildings controlled by him to install the dishes or indoor systems. Richard Li also banned WTT HK Limited from entering the large residential areas and buildings built and managed by Cheung Kong to install cable TV.

This perfectly demonstrated the old saying: "All the hustle and bustle in the world is for profit."

Li Ka-shing and Yue-Kong Pao were good friends, and they'd had joint interests in the past, involving WTT HK Limited and China Building. But today, they did not want to be involved in the younger generation's competitive battles. The fathers decided to step aside, leaving Peter Woo and Richard Li to handle everything.

However, Li Ka-shing and Richard Li did not expect that apart from cable TV, the income of TVB would also be significantly affected by the rollout of satellite TV. As a result, the three companies jointly put pressure on the Hong Kong government. In December 1990, the government issued a business license to the satellite TV, with two strings attached. First, Cantonese programs were not allowed to be broadcast. Second, they were not allowed to charge users.

This was a depressing turn for Li and his son. Although Asian satellites could provide television and telecommunications services to more than 30 countries and regions, the main market was in Hong Kong. The city's population was unwilling to watch Mandarin programs; most of them couldn't even understand Mandarin. Prohibiting satellite TV from broadcasting Cantonese programs was, in effect, to ask it to give up the Hong Kong market.

In March 1991, the Satellite Television Company was established with Li Ka-shing as Chairman, and Simon Murray and Richard Li as Vice Chairmen. The competition between satellite TV, cable and wireless reached such a pitch that Li Ka-shing and his son took a number of dramatic measures. With the help of the media, they accused the Hong Kong government of issuing ridiculous regulations, claiming that not allowing a local television station to broadcast programs in a local language was unreasonable.

Li also employed an independent public relations company to conduct an opinion poll. It found that 100% of satellite TV users believed that his company should broadcast Cantonese programs. (Foreign users proposed an increase in English programs.) Richard Li submitted the survey results to the Broadcasting, Culture and Sport Bureau, and to the Broadcasting Authority, hoping that public opinion would help push through rule changes.

After a series of negotiations, the Hong Kong government finally implemented a more flexible policy. It would relax the restrictions on Cantonese programs but only cable TV could charge fees.

In April 1991, the satellite TV service was launched. By the end of that year, it had used five channels to broadcast programs to users in Asia and the Pacific Islands.

Richard Li was ambitious and wanted to be a media magnate. Li Ka-shing also set him free and let him monopolize all the sectors of satellite TV.

During that time, Richard seemed to be immersed in TV. In his office, there was a wall, which consisted of 24 TV sets. He watched many programs offered by other stations and his own satellite TV station at the same time. By doing so, he could be inspired and spot the errors of his satellite service. He had a big competitive advantage, which was sheer coverage area. Satellite TV could continuously broadcast programs to more than 40 countries and regions, 24 hours a day. However, the quality of the programs was the key, since this is what would attract cash-paying advertisers.

Richard, with his unique perspective, steadily improved the quality of satellite TV programs and attracted large and larger audiences. Within 20 months, advertising revenue reached US$360 million, while operating expenses amounted to US$80 million. His business was doing well.

Of course, they never forgot the role of media. They used newspapers to advertise cartoons that satirized the government's broadcast regulations.

On 2 July 1992, the Hong Kong government finally promulgated a new set of radio and television regulations. It announced that satellite TV could start broadcasting Cantonese programs by the end of October 1993. However, satellite TV could not operate pay-TV independently; it had to do so by setting up charging programs on cable channels.

This regulatory change not only lifted the ban on TV programmes, but also encouraged Richard Li to make peace with Peter Woo. The two resolved their disputes, divided their spheres of operation and formed an alliance.

When all was settled, Richard Li made a grand move. He sold his satellite TV stake to a global media magnate. This deal brought the Li family and Hutchison Whampoa HK$1.5 billion each.

'Superman Li Junior' became famous after this, and the *Hong Kong Economic Times* commented: "Young people are worthy of admiration! Li Ka-shing's second son, Richard Li, finally made a good show this time. He brought nearly HK$3 billion to Hutchison Whampoa and his father ... Li Ka-shing hopes for his son to succeed, and now he gets what he hoped for."

At the end of August 1993, Richard Li was appointed Vice Chairman of Hutchison Whampoa. This was the reward for his success in satellite TV, and there was no objection among the business' leadership. He was 27 years old that year.

Surprisingly, Richard soon announced the establishment of his own private company, Pacific Century Regional Developments Limited.

Li Ka-shing did not oppose this move by his son, forever a lone ranger. "Young people have their own dreams and Hutchison Whampoa has enough managing staff," he said, "so I will not force him to stay here."

4. LI KA-SHING FOUNDATION

In Li Ka-shing's office, there was a couplet written by Zuo Zongtang, a famous official from the late Qing Dynasty, reading: "Aim high, contain oneself and live by simplicity; achieve most, balance oneself and behave with tolerance."

This was perhaps Li Ka-shing's motto, as it was certainly the rule he lived his life by and was his strategic key to dealing with others.

Many people can make money, but to become truly human, like Li Ka-shing, required a lot of practice. Diligence, frugality and honesty were his virtues. Calmness was his chief characteristic. Flexibility and determination were the reflection of his will. His wisdom allowed him to advance and withdraw appropriately, and imparted him with the importance of modesty and courtesy.

Effective management of his subordinates and cooperation with his rivals showed his broad-mindedness and tolerance. In addition, donating the money he had pursued all his life provided a window into his soul.

To that end, in 1980 the Li Ka-shing Foundation was established.

"The foundation is like a third son of mine," Li proclaimed, "and one day it will account for more than one third of my property."

The money that he had donated went to charitable causes. However, Li Ka-shing cautioned its employees not to operate the foundation in the name of charity. Two directions were already set for its development. One was to foster people's capability through education, and the other was to establish a society of care through investing in medical treatment and relevant projects.

The records reflect that the Li Ka-shing Foundation has donated money to many projects, with 64% of its funds going to improving educational, medical and cultural undertakings in mainland China.

Li also had his own unique views on aid for students. As for educational programmes in the western regions, he believed that if there was no 'leap-forwards' progress in people's thinking, the donated resources would not be efficiently used.

His approach was to provide teachers and students in the western regions with access to qualified distance education from developed regions through satellites and the internet. To this end, he spent 300 million yuan to equip 10,000 primary and secondary schools and 13 universities with the internet and satellite network access. Some 10,000 village teachers could be trained in this programme. It was expected to help rural teachers solve their problems of inadequate capability and to form an effective education system with lasting implications.

Over the past few years, the foundation's investments in education in mainland China include: Cheung Kong

Graduate School of Business; the Education and Medical Plan in Western Regions; Cheung Kong Scholars Program; the new library in Peking University; Future Internet Technology Centre in Tsinghua University; Chaozhou Elementary School; Guangdong Police College; and, most importantly, Shantou University.

Investments in medical treatment include: Shantou University Medical College; Phase I and Phase II of Care for the Disabled; Neighborhood Project of the New Milestone Program; National Hospice Service Program; Reborn Action, a cleft-palate surgical rehabilitation program for poor children; Zhongren Nursing Home in Jinshan, Shanghai; Chaozhou Central Hospital; Medical Assistance Project for Poverty Alleviation; Caring as the Tide Project; Rural Health Construction in Hainan Province; Sanitation Support in the Rural Needy Region, Shaanxi Province; Public Security and Medical Assistance Foundation for Polices in Guangdong Province; Health Express Project; and Smiling Action Project.

Li Ka-shing also donated to the cultural and artistic fields. It could be said that he invested heavily in the construction of his home town and other cities in mainland China.

After Hong Kong's return to Chinese rule, Li Ka-shing finally came back to his home town of Chaozhou. It had been 40 years since he'd left. He was very happy to see the changes in the place of his birth, but when he learned that there was no college there he decided to donate a university.

In 1981, he invested hundreds of millions of Hong Kong dollars to establish Shantou University. The deed received strong support from the Ministry of Education and the Guangdong Provincial Government. The university was built in northwest Shantou, with a total area of 1,888,70 acres.

Office buildings, dormitories, teaching buildings, laboratories and other buildings occupied an area of 4.3052 billion square metres.

In the autumn of 1983, the first phase of Shantou University's construction started. On the evening of 31 December, Li Ka-shing delivered a speech at the school's Foundation Ceremony. "I think the foundation of Shantou University is in line with public opinion and warmly welcomed by local people," he said. "I will do everything possible to make sure that this university is well constructed and operated. This is my greatest wish."

The next day, he held an international press conference. "The most advanced science, technology and machines must be managed and controlled by talents with excellent ideological and cultural qualities," he declared. "Shantou University is founded now to train talents for the four modernizations of China, and especially for the Chaoshan area. We will cultivate talents who can serve Chaoshan people, and contribute to the development of Chaoshan!"

He added, "It is my ultimate aim to support and serve the country."

On 20 June 1986, Deng Xiaoping met Li Ka-shing in the Great Hall of the People and praised his patriotic deed in building Shantou University. Deng told him and Li Tieying, Director of the State Education Commission, "Establishing Shantou University is fabulous, and it must run well. A group of excellent teachers across the country will be sent there, and it should be open and become a key national university."

During construction, officials once consulted Li Ka-shing on whether he wanted to name a building after himself or his father, Li Wan King. He declined the opportunity.

On 8 February 8 1990, Shantou University was completed. In his speech of appreciation, the school's president said: "In order to establish Shantou University, Mr Li Ka-shing not only generously donated nearly HK$600 million, but also personally participated in its planning. He spared no effort in solving problems faced by the university. Mr Li Ka-shing's contribution to improving education and strengthening our country is a milestone in the history of Chinese higher education."

There was no doubt that the school went on to live up to expectations. It focused on medicine and achieved remarkable results. There were 1,540 teaching and administrative staff and 10,056 students. In total, it trained more than 90,000 talents of all kinds for service to society. Moreover, the Ministry of Education designated it a pilot university for a new Physician Education and Training Program of Excellence.

Li Ka-shing's and Deng Xiaoping's wishes for the institution had come true.

At the end of his book, *Three Days on the Yangtze River*, the Chinese writer Liu Baiyu observed, "The sky is so soft and the water ripples like silk. Two white gulls slowly fly at the same height with the ship named 'Jiangjin.' At the far end of the horizon, the water condenses into transparent mist. Clusters of sails are like white flowers under the blue sky."

What a perfect life it is, incorporating ongoing efforts, unremitting struggles and enormous success!

When he retired at the age of 90, with a gentle wave, Superman Li said farewell to Cheung Kong Holdings, to which he had devoted his entire life. People could learn from his experience that to explore a splendid career one must plan in advance, govern systematically, resist haste and allow things to develop without interruption.

Although these expressions were simple and unadorned, to understand the essence of them and apply them in one's own life requires careful thought, practical experiences, and the unity of knowledge and action.

ABOUT THE AUTHOR

Yan Qicheng is a famous Chinese writer with the pen name of Jianggong. His long biography *Jack Ma and Alibaba* was well received by the readers at home and abroad upon publication, with sales exceeding 100,000. It was published nine times and translated into English, Italian, Arabic, Portuguese and other languages. He has also written over ten long novels and many of his TV scripts have been shot and broadcast.